The ONE-STOP Guide to

Implementing
RTI

D0774962

*I dedicate this book to my son and business partner, Marty Appelbaum,
who helped me on the RTI journey. I could not have written this book had
he not supported, encouraged, and assisted me, both in our office
and during our travels speaking to audiences across the country.*

Thank you, Marty.

The ONE-STOP Guide to

Implementing RTI

Academic and Behavioral Interventions, K-12

MARYLN APPELBAUM

A JOINT PUBLICATION

CORWIN PRESS
A SAGE Company

Appelbaum
Training Institute

For information:

Corwin Press
A SAGE Company
2455 Teller Road
Thousand Oaks, California 91320
www.corwinpress.com

SAGE Ltd.
1 Oliver's Yard
55 City Road
London, EC1Y 1SP
United Kingdom

SAGE India Pvt. Ltd.
B 1/I 1 Mohan Cooperative
  Industrial Area
Mathura Road, New Delhi 110 044
India

SAGE Asia-Pacific Pte. Ltd.
33 Pekin Street #02-01
Far East Square
Singapore 048763

Printed in the United States of America.

Library of Congress Cataloging-in-Publication Data

Appelbaum, Maryln.
  The one-stop guide to implementing RTI : academic and behavioral interventions, K–12 / Maryln Appelbaum.
      p. cm.
  "A joint publication with the Appelbaum Training Institute."
  Includes bibliographical references and index.
  ISBN 978-1-4129-6444-9 (cloth) — ISBN 978-1-4129-6445-6 (pbk.)
  1. Problem children—Education—United States. 2. Behavior disorders in children—United States. 3. Learning disabled children—Education—United States. I. Title.

LC4802.A67 2009
  371.9—dc22
                                    2008037557

This book is printed on acid-free paper.

08 09 10 11 12 10 9 8 7 6 5 4 3 2 1

Acquisitions Editor:	David Chao
Editorial Assistant:	Brynn Saito
Production Editor:	Appingo Publishing Services
Cover Designer:	Monique Hahn
Graphic Designer:	Brian Bello

Contents

List of Figures

Preface

I can still remember when I first heard the term *Response to Intervention (RTI)* many years ago. I said, "What's that?" The person who had mentioned it said, "It's going to be the next hot topic in education." He knew very little about it—just that a federal law had been passed that mentioned RTI.

That conversation stimulated my interest. I started digging around to see what I could find out about RTI. The first thing I heard was it meant that general education teachers would bear the responsibility of implementing RTI for students with difficulties within the general education classroom. My initial thoughts were, "How will they do that? They are often alone in the classroom. They are already overwhelmed. Will this overwhelm them even more?" My next thoughts were about the students. I wondered if this would really benefit them.

I then launched a super-quest. I searched on the Internet. I ordered every book that had been written on RTI. I looked at every bit of research that had been done. I read every journal article I could find. I contacted the authors of the journal articles. I attended every meeting with a speaker on RTI. I asked questions, but found that many times the speakers couldn't answer practical questions. I wanted practical information, but instead received answers that were mostly theoretical and complex. I kept digging, and the more I learned, the more I liked what I found as I sifted through the maze. I became convinced that RTI was something that would help students. My previous books and talks were all strategy-based. I was determined to write a book about RTI. I was determined to put all the information I found together in an easy-to-read format. I was fortunate to be able to visit a school district that was implementing RTI. I was even more fortunate to have a former speaker for our company who was now principal of a school that was implementing RTI. I was able to interview him and other educators around the country, and ask them what they really wanted to know about RTI.

They all said they wanted the nuts and bolts, not just the theory. They knew they had to do it. They just wanted to know how to do it, and do it right. They wanted to know how to create collaborative teams that want to implement RTI. They wanted to know more about students with learning disabilities. They wanted to know academic and behavioral research-based interventions. They wanted to know how to continually progress monitor students in the least time consuming, but accurate, ways.

That is what this book is about. It is the nuts and bolts. Yes, there will be some explanations about RTI, its history, and the basic fundamentals, but they will be brief and all tied in to practical how-to's so that when you finish reading this book, you can implement RTI in your school or classroom.

It is my personal belief that RTI is one of the best and most important strategies in education. It will literally transform schools in the United States. It will help students succeed in ways that no other legislation has done. In the end, not only will the students be more successful, but the schools will be more successful as well. And our society will be a better place for children because they will have succeeded, thanks to RTI.

Acknowledgments

Thank you to everyone at Corwin Press for your encouragement and support during the writing of this book. Special thanks goes to David Chao, my editor. Your enthusiasm and direction were wonderful. Allyson Sharp, thank you. Your support through my writing of this book was so helpful and special to me. You even called me while you were on maternity leave! Special thanks also to Lisa Allen for your hard work helping make this manuscript happen!

There are so many wonderful people who have helped me on my own RTI journey to write this book. Special thanks to Dr. Carol Booth from the Galena Park School District. This was the first school district I visited in my quest to learn more about RTI, and hearing about your success spurred me on to want to learn more. I especially want to thank Robert Underwood, who worked for my company and then became a principal who implements RTI. He was very helpful in giving me feedback. His enthusiasm over the benefits of RTI helped me to be even more enthusiastic. Thanks also to Kathy Baker, Principal of Ponderosa Elementary School in Post Falls, Idaho, for sharing your positive RTI experiences, and special thanks to the countless other administrators and teachers who shared your experiences with RTI with me. I had many questions, and you gave me answers that helped pave the way for this book to be written.

Thank you to all of the wonderful people who did not know me personally, but offered help when I contacted them for information about RTI. Special thanks to Carl Liaupsin, Associate Professor and Director of Emotional and Behavioral Disorders Program, University of Arizona; Sarah Short, at the National Center on Student Progress Monitoring; George Sugai, PhD, Codirector, OSEP Center on Positive Behavioral Interventions and Support; Heather George, PhD, Assistant Professor and Program Coordinator for Florida's Positive Behavior Support Project; Laura Riffel, PhD; and Rachel Freeman, PhD, Research Professor at the University of Kansas. Thank you to Ed Kame'enui, PhD, and Dean Knight, Professor of Education, at the University of Oregon.

During the writing of this book I contacted many additional names well known in the field of education and most especially RTI. Many of their names are listed in the references for research journals. Special thanks goes to all of these people who took the time to answer e-mails, talk to me on the phone, and send additional links, journal articles, and information on the implementation of RTI.

Thank you to those who reviewed this book. Your comments helped to make it better and more thorough.

Thank you to the fabulous audience I had in Houston when I did my first talk on RTI. One principal said, "I attended a seminar for two full days, but in one hour you have finally made clear what it is that I have to do." She had no idea how her words motivated and encouraged me to make this book user friendly for you.

And most of all, special thanks to our wonderful Appelbaum Training Institute team for all your support as together we reach out to help educators all over the world. Together, we do make a difference. Thank you.

Corwin Press gratefully acknowledges the contributions of the following reviewers:

Karen A. Brainard
Intervention Coordinator
Hilliard City School District
Hilliard, OH

Wendy Dallman
Special Education Teacher
New London High School
New London, WI

Mari Gates
Special Education Co-Teacher, Grade 5
Henry B. Burkland Intermediate School
Middleboro, MA

Beth Madison
Principal
George Middle School
Portland, OR

About the Author

 **Maryln Appelbaum** is well known internationally as an outstanding authority on children, education, and families. She has master's degrees in both psychology and education and completed her doctoral studies in both education and psychology. She has worked as a teacher, administrator, and therapist, and has been a consultant throughout the United States. She has written more than thirty "how to" books geared exclusively for educators and parents. She has been interviewed on television and radio talks shows and has been quoted in newspapers, including *USA Today*.

She owns a seminar training company, Appelbaum Training Institute, with her son, Marty Appelbaum, and they and their speakers train educators all over the world.

Maryln's influence impacts the entire globe with her "Thoughts for the Day" that are sent via e-mail to thousands of educators all over the world every day. Her strategies have been implemented in schools across the world successfully. There is not a day that goes by that someone does not contact her at Appelbaum Training Institute to tell her "thank you." Those "thank you's" come from teachers, administrators, parents, and students whose lives have been impacted by Maryln.

Maryln is a pro at Response to Intervention. She speaks often on RTI to educators across the nation, helping them understand and implement RTI in their schools. She knows the ins and outs of RTI. All her books are strategy-based, and her book and talks on RTI are the same. She believes in RTI as a powerful method for helping schools and students succeed. She is enthusiastic, dynamic, dedicated, and caring—a one-of-a-kind difference maker for the world.

Introduction

RTI is going to completely restructure American education in ways that we have never seen before. As I travel through the country speaking, I hear over and over how our schools are failing children and how American education is lagging behind other countries. This will all change with the implementation of RTI. Students have struggled for years. Students have dropped out because of academic and behavior problems. Many behavior problems were actually caused by learning problems. When students cannot learn, they become frustrated. The more frustrated they become, the more likely they are to misbehave. RTI has the potential to revolutionize all this. There will be no more students waiting to fail. There will be no more teachers frustrated because they have a "feeling" something is wrong with a particular student, but they just can't seem to get a handle on how to reach that student. Now, they will know.

Change is not easy. As a matter of fact, the one thing that people often fear is change. Change means restructuring or revamping old ways. It means thinking and acting in new ways. From every struggle there can emerge new meaning. I am thinking now as I write this of Martin Luther King, Jr., and his message of having a dream. He wanted to overcome racism. He wanted equality for all. His dream meant change. His dream continues to come true, not only in America but all over the world. I, too, have a dream. I believe that RTI is the vehicle for making that dream come true, not only in America, but all over the world.

I write "Thoughts for the Day" for educators who subscribe to receive them via e-mail all over the world. In 2007 I wrote my dream for education. Thanks to RTI, I believe this dream will now come true.

"I have a dream."

Martin Luther King said these powerful words. I, too, have a dream.

I dream of the day when teachers will be acknowledged, honored, and respected for the key roles they play in building the future.

I dream of the day when parents will look at you who work with their children and realize how important your work and your influence are in the lives of their children. They will respect you and want to work together as a team on behalf of their children.

I dream of the day when you will walk inside a room filled with people and when someone says, "What do you do?" and you respond, "I'm a teacher," they will applaud you and thank you for the important work you do.

I dream of the day when students will come into your schools and classrooms with respect.

I dream of the day when no student falls through the cracks, but instead all students succeed.

I dream of the day when families will realize that the most valuable asset that they have is their children.

I dream of the day when your voice counts—when people across the world know that you are the backbone of society—the ones that build the future of the world every day with the important work you do.

I dream of the day when together we show the world how important you are, and this dream comes true!

Response to Intervention (RTI)

The Major Shift in Education

1

RTI has the potential to revolutionize education so that no child really ever falls behind.

—Maryln Appelbaum

Throughout the years there have been many innovations in education; however, I believe none can compare to Response to Intervention (RTI). RTI has the potential to totally transform the face of education. When I do seminars all over the country, I hear over and over again statements like, "Students can't sit still anymore," "I have to play the part of policeman," "I have more students than ever before who are defiant and disinterested," and "Students today just don't learn like they used to." Educators are complaining. They tell me they want to be able to reach students so they can learn. RTI is the process that will help this happen.

RTI started with the reauthorization of the Individuals with Disabilities Education Act (IDEA) in 2004 (Bradley, Danielson, & Doolittle, 2007). Up until this law was passed, students with learning disabilities were generally first identified using the "discrepancy model." If there was a discrepancy between a student's IQ and the student's achievement, this was cause for alarm. Often this discrepancy was not found until the student had been in school for several grades.

This discrepancy model for learning disabilities (LD) evaluation led to misidentifying students with LD (Harry & Klingner, 2007). A student with a higher IQ who had insufficient knowledge of English would often score lower on achievement tests. Students who had a hard time focusing, students who were unmotivated, and students with limited vocabularies were also at risk of being identified as learning disabled because of their low achievement scores.

The reauthorized IDEA changed all of this. The discrepancy model was not forgotten, but now there was new wording—wording that spoke about using a process to help students through scientific research-based interventions as part of an evaluation procedure (Wedl, 2005). The reauthorized act now said that to determine a Learning Disability the local education agency did not need to take into consideration a discrepancy between achievement and intellectual ability (IDEA, 2004). Now local education agencies (LEAs) could adopt alternative models of identification (Wedl, 2005).

OUT WITH THE OLD—THE DISCREPANCY MODEL

Can you remember starting kindergarten? There was probably some fear, and yet there was a feeling of being grown up and a hope for the future. Students with learning disabilities start school alongside their peers with that same fear and hope. But then something happens along the way. The students with learning disabilities begin to struggle. Their teachers in kindergarten and the early grades may notice something is wrong, but usually nothing is done until third or fourth grade (Fletcher, Coulter, Reschly, & Vaughn, 2004). That is when students take tests. Their scores from IQ tests do not match up with achievement test scores. Now these students are noticed and referred for testing. After extensive and expensive testing, many of these students are often diagnosed as having learning disabilities and are referred for special education. This was the process and is still the process in many schools.

It is a "wait to fail" model because it relies on academic failure to trigger the need for help. Valuable years in which students could have been helped earlier have been lost. The saddest part is that because it took so long to get help, many students have established patterns of thinking they cannot learn. They develop learned hopelessness (Firmin, Hwang, & Copella, 2004). It takes a lot of hard work by faculty members to convince these students that there are ways to succeed. Some students have gone on like this even longer. They completed elementary school, middle school, and high school undetected. Their teachers thought they were lazy, unmotivated, and disinterested. They often developed negative behaviors to cover up their fear of failure. They would rather have their teachers and peers think of them as "bad" than as "dumb."

RTI changes all of this. The RTI process is designed to help all children succeed, to catch students early if they have problems, and to teach in a scientifically research-based method to ensure success for all learners.

IN WITH THE NEW—THE RTI PROCESS

RTI is a step-by-step tiered process that includes systematic, research-based instruction and interventions for struggling learners. It starts in kindergarten (and in some cases, preschool) and continues through the grade levels to ensure that no child falls behind. The first tiers of the process all take place in the general education classroom with the general education teacher (Fuchs & Fuchs, 2007). It is a safe and familiar setting for students.

It is a process of providing testing to determine if students need help, the intervention, and then further testing to ensure the interventions are working (Fuchs & Fuchs, 2007). The instruction and interventions are matched to the needs of students. It is designed to be an early intervention process to prevent long-term academic failure and to help children adapt to the general education classroom.

The RTI process has two completely different aspects. There is Academic RTI, which is designed to help students with academic difficulties succeed, and there is also Behavioral RTI, sometimes called Behavioral PBIS (Positive Behavior Intervention Supports) (Fairbanks, Sugai, & Guardino, 2007).

Figure 1.1 Response to Intervention

Response to Intervention	
Academic RTI	Behavioral PBIS

UNIVERSAL SCREENING

The RTI process begins with universal screening of all students (Mellard & Johnson, 2008). The purpose of universal screening is to determine which students need help. RTI cannot begin without this screening. It lays the groundwork for the entire process. It is recommended that it take place at the beginning of the school year, and be repeated again in the winter and spring.

All students in the district are assessed. Each district chooses its own screening instruments for measuring both academics and behavior. There are screening tools that are for entire groups of students, and there are other screening instruments that are administered to individual students. The testing needs to be brief, easy to administer, reliable, and valid. The ideal universal screening is research-based. Many districts use Curriculum-Based Measurement (CBM) for academic screening (Shinn, 2007). Using CBM, the teacher gives students timed short probes of academic material in reading, writing, or math taken from the school curriculum. CBM has the advantage of being tied into the individual district's curriculum. Behavioral RTI requires different universal screening. One research-based instrument schools have used is Systematic Screening for Behavior Disorders (SSBD).

Universal screening instruments need to satisfy several important criteria. As stated before, it needs to be efficient, which means it cannot be too time consuming or expensive. Administering and scoring the instrument needs to be short and accurate. This requires that the data is not difficult to interpret.

Another important criteria is that it needs to be a good instrument for classifying students at risk or not at risk in whatever area is being screened. It must also determine cut scores to be used. Cut scores are cut points that represent the dividing line between students who are not at risk and students who are potentially at risk (Mellard & Johnson, 2008).

Screening instruments may be criterion-based or norm-based (Aviles, 2001). Criterion-based instruments show a level of proficiency on the skill being measured, such as reading. The criterion referenced is to a standard rather than to the achievement of other students. Normative referenced screening compares results to other similar peer groups. For example, students in a class in a grade level may be compared to peers in the same grade level. Criterion-based screening instruments are generally preferred because they are thought to give more comprehensive and accurate information about specific skills.

Ideally there would be more than one instrument used for screening. A battery of screening instruments would enhance the accuracy of the screening (Jenkins & O'Connor, 2002). When teachers rate the behavior and attentiveness of students, this too enhances accuracy (Davis, Lindo, & Compton, 2007). In addition, the instrument used would match the instruments used for monitoring progress of students.

I would like very much to tell you about a specific Web site that organizes all of the universal screening instruments, describing the research that has been done on them. However, at the time of this writing, there was no specific Web site available. The main reason for this is that research is still in progress. This is especially true in secondary schools. Many secondary schools have opted to use the state standardized test scores for the basis of their academic universal screening. Some combine this with attendance, previous grades, and teacher rating scales. There are several excellent sources listed in the back of this book, including the National Research Center on Learning Disabilities, the National Center on Response to Intervention, and the RTI Action Network, that will hopefully soon have information for referrals. More information and new Web sites are continually added to keep up to date with research to meet the needs of implementing RTI.

Universal screening is an important part of the RTI process. It is a comprehensive method for knowing where students stand. Once you know where they stand, you can help them. Now you can tier instruction.

TIER 1

RTI is usually described using a triangle that has three layers (Batsche, 2005). The bottom layer is Tier 1 for both academics and behavior management. This is where students are identified as needing help after the universal screening. Typically, eighty to ninety percent of students are learning fine and can continue to be taught in the regular prescribed manner. The other ten to twenty percent of students are identified as being at risk and need academic or behavioral interventions or both. These numbers can vary within school districts with some numbers being larger and some numbers being smaller. The students who need extra help (interventions) are all taught within the general education classroom using research-based interventions (Batsche, 2005). Research-based interventions are those interventions that have been validated through scientific studies.

The interventions need to be targeted to the areas that students need help with. For example, if a student needs help with reading, writing, or math fluency, the intervention needs to be designed to help the student. If the student needs help with behavior management, the intervention needs to be designed to help.

Each school has an RTI team that collaborates on interventions (Wright, 2007). The team meets and looks at data from universal screening as well as other data from the classroom teacher. After studying the data, the team, together with the general education teacher, decides on interventions for the general education teacher to make within the classroom.

Figure 1.2 RTI Tiers

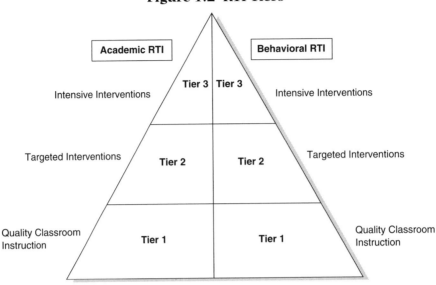

The General Education Teacher

One of the most important team members is the general education teacher (Daly, Martens, Barnet, Witt, & Olson, 2007). The general education teacher has a huge responsibility. It is the general education teacher who will be implementing the Tier 1 interventions and, in some cases, the Tier 2 interventions too (Johnson, Mellard, Fuchs, & McKnight, 2006). In order to do this, instruction for students needs to be in small groups. This is more easily accomplished through differentiated instruction. (Chapter 7 has information on how to differentiate instruction.)

It is the general education teacher that identifies students who need attention to the RTI team, establishes relationships with students, and then monitors and tracks data to determine if individual progress is being made. This is all accomplished at the same time while providing quality instruction to the rest of the class. The general education teacher is on the forefront for implementing RTI.

The Special Education Teacher

Special education teachers play an important part in the implementation of RTI as well. They have the rich experience and information needed to help design the interventions necessary for the student, and in many states, this is part of their responsibility (Johnson et al., 2006). In some districts they also help decide and/or develop measurement instruments and help collect assessment data. It is the job of special education teachers and specialists to collaborate with general education teachers to ensure the interventions are implemented correctly and with fidelity. The special education teacher is very much involved in helping students and serves as a valuable resource for general education teachers. In cases where students have not progressed satisfactorily in the first tiers, the special education teacher is generally very involved in writing and helping to implement Individualized Education Programs (IEPs) for students.

Progress Monitoring

In order to know if the interventions are effective, the progress of the students needs to be continuously monitored (Johnson et al., 2006). Interventions are only as good as the progress that is seen in students. An intervention that works for one student is not necessarily the best one for another student. Progress monitoring involves using scientifically based assessments to determine efficacy of the interventions. It begins in Tier 1 and occurs in all tiers of instruction (Mellard & Johnson, 2008).

There are two components of RTI: academic and behavior. For academic RTI, it is best if progress monitoring assesses the specific skills that are found in state and local academic standards that are therefore part of the academic content (Johnson et al., 2006). Behavioral RTI also needs to meet the behavioral objectives of the school and district. Both academic and behavioral progress monitoring needs to be relevant to the creation and use of instructional strategies that students need (National Association of State Directors of Special Education, 2005). The end result for both academic and behavioral RTI needs to be teacher-friendly so that it is easy to interpret. All progress monitoring needs to be predictive and demonstrate longitudinally what will happen in the future. It needs to be applicable to the instructional strategies that are being used to correct deficits and able to be administered repeatedly and efficiently to students over a period of time.

Ideally the instrument used for progress monitoring should match the instrument used for universal screening; however, this is not always the case. At the back of this book is a list of resources. One of those resources is a government-sponsored agency called What Works Clearinghouse. The task of What Works Clearinghouse is to provide reviews of the effectiveness of research-based products and practices. Still another resource is the National Center for Progress Monitoring, which reviews programs for progress monitoring and offers information about the programs reviewed. There are many other excellent resources for finding the best programs for progress monitoring, academic and behavioral interventions, and universal screening instruments also listed at the back of this book.

At the time of the writing of this book, there were not as many research-based academic progress monitoring programs available for secondary schools, most especially high schools; however, the list is growing all the time, and the research will soon catch up with what is needed.

Just as more than one instrument for universal screening is important, so too is more than one instrument for progress monitoring. Multiple assessment methods lead to more comprehensive assessments to determine the strengths and needs of students. Curriculum-based measurement (CBM) is often used in both universal screening and in progress monitoring for academics. The advantage of using CBM for both is that it makes it easier to determine student progress in a particular subject (Mellard & Johnson, 2008). It is tied into the school's curriculum and what students need to know. Curriculum-based measures focus on target skills. Additional teacher-developed classroom assessments can be used to target not only those content areas but across content areas to other subjects.

One of the major advantages of CBM is the simple scoring. Other types of assessments are often time-consuming and can be subjective. For example, when teachers do a one-minute reading probe to determine the number of words read correctly, the score is easily determined. The graphing provides a clear picture of baseline to target scores (Pemberton, 2003). If teachers do this once a week over a period of ten weeks, they can plot the scores on a line graph to determine progress. Figure 1.3 clearly illustrates Johnny's progress over the course of ten weeks. The target goal was sixty words per minute read correctly. Johnny reached the goal. Data like this allows a clear picture of progress or lack of progress.

A major component of implementing progress monitoring and all of RTI is professional development. It is especially important that teachers receive training in how to track data accurately (Sargent, 2001). Without this key piece, progress monitoring would be in vain.

Students are progress monitored ranging from daily to every two weeks, depending on the tier of instruction and the program. If students do not improve after a designated time period, they are moved to the next tier of instruction for more targeted or intensive interventions. If students do improve, they may return to a lower tier or remain in the same tier for more supplemental instruction.

Summary of Tier 1

- Students are taught in the general education classroom.
- At-risk students are usually identified in the first month of the school year.

Figure 1.3 Johnny's Progress

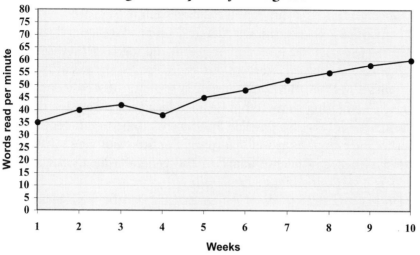

- Once a student is identified as an at-risk performer, interventions begin and student's progress is monitored through the collection and tracking of data.
- All students are given general instruction, using evidence-based instructional strategies.
- Intervention strategies are designed to be both preventative and proactive.

TIER 2

In the middle layer of the triangle described earlier is Tier 2 (Batsche, 2005). If students are not progressing in comparison to their peers and their expected ability, they need more intensive instruction and interventions. Approximately five to ten percent of students, depending on the school, generally fall into this category. Once it is determined through progress monitoring over a period of time that these students are not succeeding in Tier 1, new interventions are specifically designed for them so that they can succeed.

Their instruction in Tier 2 is usually done individually or in small groups (Batsche, 2005). Students receive their regular general instruction with the rest of the class and also supplemental instruction in any areas that are identified as being weak for them. The supplemental instruction, depending on the district and school, occurs for between thirty and ninety minutes, two to five times a week.

It is possible for students to receive Tier 1 instruction for some academic subject areas, and Tier 2 instruction for other subject areas (Cruey,

2006). For example, when Jonathon's teacher did academic progress monitoring, she found that Jonathon excelled in most aspects of reading, but he needed supplemental instruction to increase reading fluency. She consulted with the RTI intervention team, and together they designed a series of research-based interventions and supports. He was in Tier 2 several times a week for thirty minutes each session. After only one month, progress monitoring showed that he no longer needed Tier 2 supplemental instruction. It is also possible for students to be in different tiers for behavior interventions as well. The primary purpose of Tier 2 instruction is always to help students adapt to the general education classroom (Ardoin, Witt, Connel, & Koenig, 2005).

Finding the time to do the interventions can be a problem. Some schools have a special "tier time" in their schools. It is a block of time set aside daily for the different tiers. The general education teacher provides Tier 1 instruction; a specialist such as a reading or math interventionist provides Tier 2 instruction; and a special education teacher provides Tier 3 instruction. The time for Tier 3 instruction needs to be longer because it is more intensive. The different tiers can be given different names so that students do not feel like they are better or less than other students in the class.

Different schools have different models for handling the tiers and the instructors for the tiers. Some districts have extra help and send in a faculty member such as a special education instructor, an interventionist, or a trained paraprofessional to help. Still other districts hire retired teachers on a part-time basis to help the general education teacher. However, in many schools there may not be funding for special help, and the general education teacher is responsible for implementation. This requires the general education teacher to thoroughly understand and know how to implement the intervention and differentiated instruction. Differentiated instruction is a research-based process for meeting the needs of all learners (Sullivan, 1993).

Summary of Tier 2

- If students are not progressing in comparison to peers and expected ability, instruction is supplemented with academic interventions.
- If students are not progressing behaviorally, additional behavioral interventions are administered.
- Students move in and out of Tier 2 as needed.
- Students receive instruction individually or in small groups.

- Students may be in Tier 1 for some subjects or behaviors and in Tier 2 for others. Once the subject matter or behavior is mastered, students return to Tier 1.
- Students receive general instruction plus supplemental instruction in the identified weak areas for thirty to ninety minutes, two or five times a week for a period of five to eight weeks.

TIER 3

If students do not make progress in Tier 2, they move to the top of the triangle, or Tier 3. Approximately one to five percent of students need the intensive interventions that are required at this level (Batsche, 2005). These students need more individualized instruction and learning supports. Tier 3 interventions are much more individualized and generally involve very small groups or one-on-one time with a specialist who is often a special education instructor (Cruey, 2006).

The goal is to help students get out of Tier 3 and back into one of the lower tiers. Students in Tier 3 are progress monitored on a more frequent regular basis. If they are not making progress, they are generally referred for testing at this point. For districts that have more tiers, students simply keep getting more and more intensive interventions with each progressive tier of instruction (Mellard & Johnson, 2008).

If students do not succeed at the highest tier of instruction, then students may have a disability. An IEP meeting is called to get permission to evaluate the student (Stecker, 2007). The IEP team may find when reviewing all the data and documentation that there was some type of error. There may have been lack of fidelity in the interventions, meaning they were not administered appropriately. They may even find errors in scoring for progress monitoring. If they do find any errors, the student is referred back to previous tiers for further interventions. If everything was done correctly, then the IEP team will get permission to evaluate the student to determine eligibility for special education (McCook, 2006).

It is at this point that the role of the special education teacher becomes even more important. It is generally the special education teacher's responsibility to identify students who need more intensive interventions and progress monitoring, and it is therefore the special education teacher who coordinates the next steps with parents or guardians (Johnson et al., 2006). Often, the special education teacher becomes an advocate for students to ensure they are all given important consideration prior to any decisions about placements, further evaluation, and interventions and strategies.

Summary of Tier 3

- If students are not progressing as expected after Tier 2 intervention, they are moved to Tier 3.
- Tier 3 interventions are typically more individualized and involve very small group or one-on-one time with a specialist.
- Most students will receive special education services.
- Individualized interventions are assessment-based and are called intensive.
- The instruction is highly intensive and may last thirty to 180 minutes for a designated period of time.
- Students are referred for special education eligibility.

FIDELITY AND PROFESSIONAL DEVELOPMENT

There are two other key ingredients in the RTI process: fidelity and professional development. Fidelity refers to the accuracy in carrying through implementation. If universal screening, progress monitoring, and interventions are not carried through with accuracy, there is no way of verifying the effectiveness. To ensure fidelity, there needs to be professional development. This ensures that each aspect of RTI is carried out accurately. Professional development includes not only assessment and monitoring, but also effective intervention plans and ensuring that those plans are delivered as they were written in the times that they were intended. Many schools not only need the basics of RTI but training in differentiating instruction to meet the needs of all learners in the early tiers of instruction in an effective and accurate manner. RTI is a process. It does not happen overnight. It takes training, training, and more training.

HOW RTI WILL REVOLUTIONIZE EDUCATION

Make no mistake about it, RTI *will* revolutionize education. This is not just a whim, but an entire model of teaching based on solid research done by some of the leading educators and researchers in the United States (Wedl, 2005). For the first time there are clear methods for educating all children to ensure that truly no child is left behind. Although it was originally designed to help children with learning disabilities, RTI has already begun to help all children. The process of universal screening is for all children. The process of using research-based instruction and strategies is for all children who need help. The frequent collection of data to ensure learning will help all children. The act of collaboration between general education teachers, special education teachers, the administration, and other specialists will help all children who need help. All students will have regular and systematic assessment of instructional strategies to ensure that they are on target to meet local, state, and federal standards. Students will no longer remain in learning programs in which they cannot learn. There will be fewer children with IEPs. Instead, students will get help early (Cruey, 2006). Their voices will be heard. Their voices will be heard in the data and in the tiered levels of instruction. Their voices will be heard in their improved learning (Wedl, 2005).

Framework for RTI Collaboration and Teamwork

2

Educators are the anchors for their students on the ship called Hope.
—Maryln Appelbaum

I have a personal story to share that illustrates the concepts of collaboration and teamwork. My mother and father came from two completely different countries. My mom was born in Czechoslovakia. My dad was born in Romania. Each of these countries had completely different languages and customs. My parents came separately to the United States, but they both had a common goal, and it was that they wanted to live a better life. They met each other and, in spite of the differences in languages and customs, they fell in love and got married. They had to find a way to speak a common language, to bridge their individual customs, and to work together to build their marriage. It's easy to get married. It's harder to make it a good marriage.

Working together on behalf of students in a school is a lot like a marriage. The educators in schools often come from different backgrounds and cultures. These cultures and backgrounds may be very diverse, yet they have to unite, just like in a marriage. Essentially, once each educator enters the school system, they become "married." They, like my parents, are part of a brand new culture. They become cocreators; a team working together on behalf of children. Before, they may have been accustomed to thinking of themselves, or thinking in terms of "my, mine, and I." However, once in this "school marriage," they now have to think in terms of "we and our." They have to bridge the gap of backgrounds and find a new common language to work with students.

This is a major difference from the way education worked before RTI. Yes, there were some schools where teachers cotaught and collaborated. In some cases people worked together effectively, but RTI requires even more. It requires teamwork like never before. It is essential for RTI to be effective. No one can do it alone. The administration can have the best strategies for success, but they cannot implement them alone. Each person brings their own special talents and resources to help create success on behalf of students.

There are many different people involved in implementing RTI (National Research Council on Learning Disabilities, 2008). The district begins the process. In the early stages of implementation, some districts begin with only a few schools prior to implementation throughout the entire district. The district has a huge responsibility in implementation. It is the district that allocates the resources, sets the policies and procedures, funds the program, and names the contact person(s) to work with the individual schools. These key district individuals work with principals and other key staff members within the schools to make important decisions (Johnson et al., 2006).

DISTRICT AND SCHOOL LEADERSHIP DECISIONS

All of the individuals in charge, both at the district and school level, need to be enthusiastic and knowledgeable. I have often said at workshops, "Enthusiasm is more contagious than a cold." That is true. The leader sets the tone. I can remember years ago owning four private schools. They were very successful, and I had a huge waiting list. I was enthusiastic and also knowledgeable, always keeping up with the latest trends and strategies for faculty and children. Then my personal world fell apart. My marriage of more than twenty-five years dissolved, and it affected my work life. I started seeing problems in the schools. My own personal enthusiasm and strong leadership were not there. I learned a valuable lesson from this experience. The lesson was that regardless of what is happening in one's personal life, it is imperative to leave those problems on the doorstep when you step into school. Once I understood this, the schools once again thrived.

The other key ingredient is knowledge. RTI is new. It is essential that leaders, teams, and all faculty members have the knowledge they need to implement RTI. It has to be presented in a way that is clear and understandable. Forms and paperwork have to be clear and easy to complete. Knowledge truly is power. The more everyone knows, the more easily everyone can be involved.

Screening Instruments and Research-Based Programs

The district has to make many important decisions as RTI is implemented (Johnson et al., 2006). One of the biggest decisions is to select, in conjunction with other school team members, the most appropriate tools and methods for universal screening and progress monitoring for the different grade levels. Research-based academic and behavioral programs are other key decisions. Everything needs to be coordinated to meet federal and state laws.

Forms and Paperwork

Forms and paperwork for implementation need to be designed for the schools to use. This, in itself, is a big job. They need to be simplified wherever possible. RTI takes a lot of time for teachers to implement. Schools and districts need to ensure that all laws are followed, but at the same time, use what I call the "Simplify Rule." That means the paperwork needs to be written in clear terms and be as easy and quick to complete as possible.

Professional Development

Professional development is an important key to ensuring success with RTI (National Research Council on Learning Disabilities, 2008). RTI is new and complex. It needs to be simplified so that everyone understands the process and methods. General education teachers may be concerned because they feel their responsibilities have increased. Special education teachers may be concerned about their own roles now because so much of RTI is within the realm of the general education teacher. Everyone needs training. General education teachers need training in implementation procedures, universal screening, data collection, progress monitoring, and instructional interventions and strategies. It is essential that they know how to differentiate instruction to accommodate diverse learners. It is vital that teachers have training not only in academic interventions, but also in behavioral interventions. Classroom management is always an important key to effective instruction (Appelbaum, 2008). If children are not listening and paying attention, they cannot learn. This needs to be a vital component in professional development.

Moreover, professional development needs to be presented in a way that is energizing and motivating, as well as informative (Holloway, 2003). If it is torture for the faculty to attend staff development training, and they are counting the hours until it is done, they are probably not gaining much from it. Professional development needs to be geared to meet the needs of all learners: visual, auditory, and tactile. It needs to include demonstrations, exercises, and role-playing so that faculty members can see RTI in action. This is especially true in the area of progress monitoring. Teachers need to learn how to use assessment instruments and practice collecting and translating data for progress (Johnson et al., 2006).

Other district tasks include the following:

- Scheduling time for data collection and analysis
- Informing all school personnel of RTI
- Informing parents and family members of RTI
- Providing needed resources and materials
- Budgeting time and money

RTI SCHOOL TEAMS

Once all of these are in place, it is time for the schools to take action. Schools need to have their own RTI teams (Mellard & Johnson, 2008). School teams will vary according to the size and personnel at the school. It is not the size of the team that counts as much as the effectiveness of the team. A team may have fewer members and get more done. The general functions of the RTI team are to discuss students who are struggling, help design intervention plans, and to meet as needed to re-evaluate and assess the effectiveness of the interventions.

The number of team members may also vary according to the tiers or for reviewing interventions. For example, when students are on Tier 3 and may need special education referrals, the team may increase in size. There may be members who only meet with the team once a month to review what the rest of the team has been implementing. This may be someone from the school or even from within the district.

RTI TEAM CHARACTERISTICS

The RTI team needs to share some important characteristics. They all need to share a commitment to the process of RTI (McCook, 2006). They are going to be the "cheerleaders" for the entire school. They also need to be knowledgeable about the RTI process, organized, and efficient. It is very important that they know how to read and interpret data, because they will be receiving data to review. A key characteristic is their ability to communicate. They have to be able to listen to others, as well as express their own opinions. More important, they must be aware that different team members will all have different styles of listening and interpreting what they have heard, and they must be respectful of each other (DeJesus,

Figure 2.1 Possible RTI Team Members

Principal and/or Assistant Principal	This person provides the leadership to ensure that all of the resources and services are in place.
Reading Interventionist	This is a person who is knowledgeable about reading and language interventions.
Math Interventionist	This is a person who is knowledgeable about math interventions and interpreting data.
School Psychologist or Counselor	This is a person who understands the dynamics of behavior, understands behavioral data, and can interpret assessments.
General Education Teacher	This teacher is the representative for all the other general education teachers and is knowledgeable about interventions and differentiated instruction within the general education classroom.
Special Education Specialist	This is a specialist in special education who understands students with disabilities, as well as interventions and services for them.
Speech Therapist	This is an expert in language and its development and in the different elements of speech.
Support Personnel	This may be any other individual who the team feels is important in the implementation of RTI.

Almeida, Teixeira-Dias, & Watts, 2007). Additionally, the RTI team will be hearing and learning very private information about students and, in some cases, their families. This information must remain totally confidential (Fisher, 2008).

Some schools have formed supplemental teams to help the RTI team. The supplemental teams meet on a regular basis to address concerns about struggling students and help design intervention plans. These supplemental teams could include the following:

- Grade Level Team
- Instructional Support Team (IST)
- Child Study Team
- Literacy Team
- Content Area Team

Each of these supplemental teams may act as consultants to the RTI team. Supplemental team members have diverse duties that can include the following:

- Reviewing data
- Helping set goals
- Identifying student strengths, interests, and talents
- Designing intervention plans
- Choosing methods to measure progress

After the RTI team has met and implemented a plan, these other supplemental teams may meet again to review and monitor the intervention plans for success and then make their recommendations to the RTI team.

HOW TO BUILD STRONG TEAMS

Make Time

The first major hurdle in teambuilding is to find the time for teams to meet. The greatest plan cannot be fully and successfully implemented without taking time to organize the details. For an elementary school in a high-poverty, high-crime area, I did an inservice that had huge success with students. Every Wednesday, teachers ended their day an hour and a half early and had either a planning meeting or brought in an outside speaker to train them. Teachers all stayed for this meeting or training because it took place during regular working hours. It was not a problem of working overtime by coming in early or staying later. They did not have to get substitutes. This was the most cohesive team I have ever seen in a school. The students were all making adequate yearly progress.

Some schools plan the meetings at the beginning of the day (Wright, 2007). Team members come in the morning, but instead of heading for their classrooms thirty minutes before the bell, they go once a week to their meeting that lasts for thirty minutes. Other schools do the same thing at the end of the day when students are gone but teachers are still in school.

Meetings can also take place throughout the day during common noninstructional periods. In planning the school year, it is possible to schedule faculty so this can occur. The meetings need to be a minimum of thirty minutes to one hour. Ideally it would be best for teams to meet once a week. It has been my own experience visiting schools that the more frequently teams meet, the more cohesive the school is. This cohesiveness permeates the classrooms and the school halls and can be seen in the enthusiasm of faculty members. Time set aside for meetings fosters collaboration and teamwork.

Choose an Appropriate Setting

The meeting place is very important. Over the years I have led and been part of many team meetings. The setting makes a difference. It needs to be comfortable, but not so comfortable that people fall asleep while attending the meeting. There needs to be good lighting. A conference room is the ideal setting. If you do not have a conference room available, you can still create a conference room atmosphere by taking desks and moving them into a circle so that everyone faces each other. The room has to be private to safeguard the confidentiality of students you will be discussing. Have all the necessary paperwork ready for the participants.

Start on Time

It is important that everyone attends and is on time (Mankins, 2004). If people like to chat at the beginning of the meeting, have them arrive five minutes early. Start promptly and move right into the agenda. Send out a notice ahead of time that has the agenda. Next to each item that will be covered, show the time allotted. This helps keep everyone on track and ensures the meeting is focused and all points get covered.

There are some schools that have check-in attendance sheets for faculty members to fill in as they arrive. They write the time they arrive and the time they leave. There is something about having to write it down that helps some people arrive on time and stay for the entire meeting.

Use an Agenda

Send an agenda of what will be discussed (Mankins, 2004). Itemize the topics. An agenda keeps everyone on task. It helps set the tone for participants to leave their other work behind and be present and ready to work together on behalf of students. Include the Request for Intervention form (Figure 2.2) so all team members will have had time to think about the students they will be discussing.

Respect Diversity of Opinions

Different people have different opinions. A downfall of teams that is harmful to collaboration is for people to judge the opinions of others in a negative manner (Mankins, 2004). It creates bickering and criticism. The team's purpose becomes lost, and in the end, students lose because little is accomplished before time runs out. It is essential for effective collaboration that team members are tactful and treat each other with respect. Every voice needs to count. When one person speaks, the others listen. Make this a rule for your team. Crosstalk or neighbor chatter cut the effectiveness of teams.

Figure 2.2 Request for Intervention Form

Student Name: _____ Date: _____

Teacher: _____ Grade: _____

Dominant Language: _____ Date of Birth: _____

Person(s) requesting referral: _____

First Time Referral: Yes_____ No _____   Repeat Referral: Yes_____ No_____

Current school services in place for student: _____

_____

Directions: Rank problem areas in terms of severity, 0 to 5, with 0 being no problem and 5 being the most severe. Provide details including any test results.

___Academic Performance (low or failing grades)

- Reading

- Math

- Writing

- Other_____

___Behavior and/or Discipline

___Speech—Articulation

___Language

___Medical

___Psychological

___Other (Specify) _____

When does the problem occur ? _____

Are there situations that make the problem worse? _____

_____

What interventions and strategies have you tried? _____

_____

Describe three strengths or talents of the student. _____

_____

Which school personnel would you like to have present at a meeting for the student? _____

What time of day would an RTI team member most observe the student having the problems described above? _____

Thank you for your help. Together, we are a team working together for our students.

Figure 2.3 Team Member Collaboration Checklist

☐ Help establish team goals

☐ Have an agenda

☐ Be tactful

☐ Treat each other with respect

☐ Do not talk behind the backs of others

☐ Offer opinions

☐ Disagree respectfully

☐ Encourage others on the team to voice their opinions

☐ Put your total attention on the speaker

☐ Ask questions to clarify understanding

☐ Compromise after discussion

☐ Look for consensus

☐ Share the blame if decisions turn out to be ineffective

☐ Strive to do your best

☐ Be trustworthy

☐ Complete assignments

☐ Help summarize points that are made

☐ Be respectful of ideas that conflict with your own

☐ Be enthusiastic about working together

☐ Support others who have larger tasks or busier schedules

☐ See the other person's perspective

Figure 2.4 "It Is Effective—It Works!"

Academic or Behavioral Problem	Research-Based Intervention

Promote Compromise

If a team member disagrees with another member, it needs to be done respectfully. The important thing is to look for consensus and be able to compromise. Remember, this is like a marriage. A marriage without compromise is a doomed marriage. Partners have to give and take, and so, too, do team members working together on behalf of children.

THE ROLE OF THE GENERAL EDUCATION TEACHER AND THE RTI TEAM

RTI involves a major change for general education teachers. They used to handle students with problems in the seclusion of their classrooms. They still will, but now those same struggling students are the focus of many other educators in the school. Moreover, they have to assess students often and implement interventions that may be new and uncomfortable. Some teachers may feel awkward coming to the RTI team with these problems. This was their job, and now it seems very different.

Our school is a powerful sharing and caring team of faculty that cares for students. Please add your favorite research-based intervention that is working for one of your students to the list below to share with our school team.

Have you ever bought a brand new piece of equipment? I recently purchased a new stereo for my home. I had owned the old one for over ten years. I was so excited about the new one, until I tried to work it. It was totally different. It was set up in my living room like the old one, but I had no clue how to operate it. The book was a maze of instructions. I can honestly tell you that it did nothing for my self-esteem when I could not figure out how to work it. I had someone come from the store where I bought it to help me. He gently and patiently walked me through the steps to make it work. It is the same with teachers. They are accustomed to handling students on their own in their own classrooms. They still will be handling them in their room, but now it will be like having a brand new stereo with lots of controls. Not only are the administration and RTI team involved, but often families are involved too, and this puts additional pressure on teachers to succeed with struggling students. These are a lot of changes and new responsibilities. Teachers will need a lot of help through this process, and the RTI team can assist them by being patient and understanding.

Teachers need to feel comfortable and included when they refer a struggling student. They will need guidance and professional development in implementing the interventions because some of them will be totally new and foreign. If they have never individualized instruction, they may feel very awkward. Here are some ways to help classroom teachers:

- Start an RTI "virus." A virus is something that spreads from person to person. They all catch it. In this case, the virus will be RTI. The more excited teachers and faculty become about it, the more the "virus" will spread. Pop little messages into teachers' mailboxes telling them how grades are improving in other districts because of RTI. Add RTI research-based interventions to their mailboxes—a new one every week. Some teachers will see that they may have already been implementing some of these ideas.

- Do demonstrations of RTI interventions. A picture is worth a thousand words. Help them to see what the interventions look like.

- Do demonstrations of progress monitoring. Guide them through it step-by-step (Zimmerman & Ringle, 1981). The ideal way is to explain the process. Next, model the process, talking about it as you do it. Do it again without talking. Give them a written list of the steps you are taking for them to see as you demonstrate. Now it is time to have them do it. As you watch, be sure to not focus as much on what they are doing wrong, but instead on what they are doing right. If you see an error, explain the process, demonstrate, and then have them practice again.

- Meet with teachers on a regular basis. Teachers will start to expect to see someone, and familiarity opens the doors for more communication. The more you know about their students, the more you will be able to help.

- Invite teachers to be "guests" at RTI team meetings so they can see the process in action. In this case, familiarity reduces fear of the unknown.

- Have teachers share the interventions they find most effective on an "It Works" checklist (see Figure 2.4). The list goes around the school, and teachers add their favorite research-based interventions that are effective for their students.

- Many teachers have expertise in different areas. Ask teachers with any specialized training or expertise to give input to the RTI team.

- Ask teachers who are seeing success in their classrooms with RTI to write a short article to include in faculty meetings or faculty newsletters.

- Invite teachers from other schools that are using RTI to share their success with the RTI process at faculty meetings.

- Invite teachers to become peer mentors for other faculty members in the RTI process (Wright, 2007).

RTI TEAM ROLES

There are several key roles that help RTI teams function more effectively. These roles can either be permanently assigned, or they can rotate on a regular basis. The roles are facilitator, recorder, and RTI case manager (Montana Office of Public Instruction, 2008).

The Team Facilitator

The facilitator needs to be a person who is familiar with RTI, but also is adept at collaboration and problem solving. It is the facilitator who sets the tone for creating a supportive, enthusiastic atmosphere for working together. The facilitator also has the important job of keeping the team on task, which means keeping track of time. It is the facilitator who assigns roles or gets volunteers for different responsibilities within the team.

The Recorder

The recorder also has a very important role. The recorder takes notes at the meetings, types them after the meetings so they are readable, and distributes them to all team members. The notes need to be detailed so that anyone who missed a meeting will be able to read and clearly understand the decisions made.

The RTI Case Manager

Referring teachers need a liaison on the RTI team. The case manager is the liaison—the point person to ensure that team members have all the information they need about students who are referred. This may mean consulting with the referring teacher to get additional information about the student that could be useful for the team and ensuring that the Request for Intervention form is fully completed (see Figure 2.2).

When the RTI team has met and listed interventions, it is the case manager who makes sure the referring teacher understands the interventions and is able to implement them. If there are problems with implementation, the case manager reports back to the team for additional help and support for the referring teacher.

THE RTI TEAM MEETING

Upbeat Opening

The RTI team has a very important function—to help students succeed. These team meetings can literally make or break that function. It's very important that everyone is excited about working together to help children. Start each meeting with an upbeat opening. It is very effective. Have you ever watched sports? The coach always sends the team players off with a motivating statement. That's what this team needs too. Start with an upbeat, motivational message that is unique for your team and your purpose.

Referring Teacher Report

Once the goal statement has been read, it is time to get down to business. The main business of the RTI team is to meet with referring classroom teachers and design implementation.

All team members need to have already received the Request for Intervention forms (Figure 2.2) for students who will be discussed at the meeting. This gives them time to think about what will be discussed. Referring teachers will attend the meeting and should bring additional important data that illustrates the problem. This can include copies of homework, test scores, and the completed Family Information Form for RTI Team (see Figure 2.5).

The referring teacher gives a brief overview of the academic and/or behavioral problems with the student. The teacher also provides a list of the student's talents, strengths, and likes and dislikes, so they can be used in designing interventions for the student.

Set Positive Student Goals and Time Line for Achieving Success

The next step in the process is for the entire team to set a positive goal for the student. This keeps the focus not on the problem, but on the method to achieve success. Goal setting with a time line for success allows this to happen. The goal needs to be simple and clear and should have a time line for the result.

Intervention Plan

The next step is a fundamental key to success. It is to design the Intervention Plan (see Figure 2.6). This includes a list of research-based interventions (Wright, 2007).

Figure 2.5 Family Information Form for RTI Team

Student Name_____ Student ID No._____

Family Member's Name_____ Daytime Phone _____

What is your relationship to the student? _____

Who is the legal guardian of the student? _____

Your daytime phone _____

Daytime phone of legal guardian _____

Have any of the student's classroom teachers at any time indicated any concerns about academic performance or behavior? Yes_____ No___ If yes, please describe: _____
_____

Does the student have any physical or emotional health problems?

Yes___ No___ If yes, please describe: _____
_____

Has the student ever had any psychological or learning assessments?

Yes__ No___ If yes, answer these questions. Date(s) of evaluation(s) _____

Who did the evaluation? _____

Describe the evaluation: _____

Can we see a copy of the evaluation? Yes___ No___

What were the results of the evaluation? _____
_____

Are there any situational factors occurring at home that may be influencing the child's learning or behavior? Yes___ No___

If yes, please describe: _____

Are you having any problems with the child at home right now?

Yes___ No___ If yes, please describe. _____
_____

What instructional strategies do you think will help your child? _____
_____

What strategies do you use that are effective for your child? _____
_____
_____

What strategies do you use that are not effective for your child? _____
_____
_____

How would you describe your child? _____

Signature of person completing form _____

Your relationship to child_____ Date _____

Figure 2.6 Intervention Plan Form

Student's Name _____ Date _____ Intervention will start on _____ Intervention will conclude on _____ *
Target Behavior(s)
Intervention(s)
Person(s) Implementing Intervention
Location for Implementing Intervention
Regularly Scheduled Times of Intervention
Form(s) of Progress Monitoring
Frequency of Progress Monitoring
Person(s) Progress Monitoring
This is subject to change depending on progress of the intervention.

The Role of the General Education Teacher

It is important to consider the general education teacher's views on implementing the interventions. I have found that teachers, like their students, each have their own unique styles. Some interventions may fit into their unique styles more easily than others. If the teacher is comfortable, the intervention has a better chance for success. However, there may also be some discomfort initially in using new interventions. A teacher accustomed to teaching in a whole-class lecture format may find it difficult initially to begin differentiating instruction to accommodate the needs of diverse struggling learners. This is OK. The teacher will need support through the process.

There may be some cases in which it is not the general education teacher providing the intervention. This needs to be decided at this time. It could be that the general education teacher does not have the time to do the intervention, or it could be something more specialized that calls for someone else to help. The Intervention Plan needs to spell this out.

Location of Intervention

The location for the intervention has to be chosen. Most of the time it will be in the general education classroom, but there may be times when this is not feasible. All of this has to be included in the plan.

Time and Duration of Intervention

Another important aspect of the plan is the time. The plan needs to spell out the time of day that the intervention will occur, and the duration of the intervention. It also needs to spell out approximately how long the Intervention Plan will be used. They are generally implemented for eight to twelve weeks. This is subject to change if the intervention is not working.

Progress Monitoring

In order to know if the Intervention Plan is working, the RTI team has to select a method of progress monitoring for the interventions. The screening instruments need to be chosen. Often the school and/or district will have already had input as to which instruments are preferred.

Person(s) Doing Progress Monitoring

There are other decisions to be made. The team has to decide who will be responsible for doing the actual progress monitoring. Will it be the general education teacher? Will a team member come into the classroom to do this? If it is someone other than the referring teacher, it has to be a person who is familiar to the student. If not, what I call the "fear factor" will enter the equation. Students already fear over-testing. There is comfort in familiarity even if that familiar person is the one administering a test. Someone strange administering the test can create anxiety and fear in the student, and this can cause him or her to not do as well when assessed. Ideally, the form of progress monitoring will be brief and administered by someone with whom the student is familiar.

Tracking the Data

Another concern is to choose an individual who will chart the data collected when progress monitoring. This can be the general education teacher, a team member, or even someone else within the school. Some teachers may not like to handle this mathematical component. They feel they were hired to teach, and the less paperwork the better. The problem is that this form of paperwork is really helpful for the student. It is what will show or not show the student's progress. If there is no progress, something else will need to be done. Ultimately it is all about student success or failure. It all starts with teachers and teams working together collaboratively to ensure this happens.

Including Families

Families need to be informed each step of the way about what is happening. Parents may attend the RTI planning meetings on behalf of their children. It is very helpful if parents are able to fill out the Family Information Form for the RTI Team (see Figure 2.5) so you know more about their children. Sometimes an academic or behavioral problem may be situational. The family may be going through a divorce or other trauma. Some students may have been tested somewhere else for an ongoing problem, but the school never found out. The more you know, the more you will be able to help students. The goal is to keep families in the loop and to be a team working together for their children. See Figures 2.7, 2.8, 2.9, and 2.10 for forms to include families in the learning loop.

Figure 2.7 Parent Letter: Introduction to RTI

Dear Parent,

Your child's success is important to us. Our goal is to ensure effective learning so that your child will have a positive learning experience.

Every child is unique. Every child learns differently. Every student behaves differently. Different children need different academic and behavior strategies and interventions for success. In order to meet the needs of all students, we have implemented three tiers of support. In the first tier, classroom teachers use strategies and materials for students who may need a little extra help. In the second tier, we create an individual support plan with additional interventions to help students in any specific weaker learning or behavioral areas. In each tier, the student is monitored closely to ensure that the research-based interventions are successful.

For students who still experience difficulty, there is a third tier that provides even more intensive academic and/or behavioral support. We may alter the schedules of students to ensure that they have this help. The total goal is a successful school experience.

We are happy to have your child here and look forward to a great school year.

Sincerely yours,

_____
Principal's Signature

Figure 2.8 Parent Letter: Introduction to RTI Tier 1

Dear _____[Parent],

We want to help your child succeed. We sent you a letter at the beginning of the school year explaining our three-tier approach to helping our students. Your child, _____[child's name], will begin Tier 1 interventions on _____.

Tier I interventions are designed to give a little extra help to children who need that help within their general education classroom. An intervention team has met with your child's classroom teacher and designed a specific plan for your child. The plan includes frequent monitoring to ensure that it is effective.

If you have any questions, feel free to contact _____ at _____.

We look forward to your child's success.

Sincerely yours,

_____
Principal's Signature

Figure 2.9 Parent Letter: Introduction to RTI Tier 2

Dear _____[Parent],

We want to help your child succeed. We will be providing Tier 2 instruction to your child, _____. In Tier 1, your child's classroom teacher used additional interventions to support your child. Tier 2 will provide additional research-based interventions. Your child will receive additional targeted interventions that are designed especially for your child's success. This will begin _____ _____, and occur on a regular basis. All of the interventions are designed to help your child succeed.

If you want to talk about this, feel free to contact _____ at _____.

Together, as a team, we will help your child succeed.

Sincerely yours,

_____
Principal's Signature

Figure 2.10 Parent Letter: Introduction to RTI Tier 3

Dear _____[Parent],

We want to help your child, _____, succeed. We have been providing interventions and monitoring your child's progress. Your child began in Tier 1 with additional strategies. We then moved to Tier 2 to provide your child more targeted research-based interventions.

Now, we are going to have a Tier 3 planning meeting to discuss beginning Tier 3 interventions for your child on _____(day) at _____(time) in _____(location) of our school.

Tier 3 interventions are much more intensive so that students receive more help in the areas they need. That sometimes means altering a student's schedule with the ultimate goal of helping the student. Our goal is to help your child. We hope you can attend this meeting. We are looking forward to hearing your input about your child and working together as a team to help your child succeed.

If you have any questions, feel free to contact _____ at _____.

We look to working with you as a team on behalf of your child.

Sincerely yours,

_____
Principal's Signature

Academic Interventions

3

Literacy and Math

The more you learn, the more you know there is to learn.
—Maryln Appelbaum

Once upon a time there was a sailor named Buchanon. Buchanon loved sailing the high seas. He sailed all over the world and knew the seas well. One day, the king of the land of Meaning came to him and said, "Buchanon, I have heard there is a great treasure buried beneath the sea. I believe you can find it. Would you go seek it out for me?" Buchanon thought about it, and he said, "Yes, I will be glad to do that." He searched the seas looking for clues wherever he could, finding out how the treasure had been lost, how long it had been lost, and all the details. Sure enough, he found the treasure and brought it to the king. The king was very pleased, and wanted to give him a big reward for finding the treasure. Buchanon said to the king, "Thank you, Sire, but my reward was putting those clues together and actually finding the treasure."

This chapter is starting with this story because finding the right academic interventions for students is like seeking buried treasure. It means digging for answers. If the first tier does not work, it's digging deeper and creating a second tier. If that tier doesn't work, then there has to be more digging. This can be a long and sometimes arduous process. However, once the right interventions are found and brought into place, students can sparkle like jewels. They have brighter futures.

This is the first of three chapters to help with the implementation of academic RTI. This chapter has many interventions for literacy and some for math. Chapter 4 has additional supplemental interventions, and

Chapter 5 describes how to differentiate instruction so the academic interventions can all be used within the general education classroom.

There are many excellent programs for literacy. The Florida Center for Reading Research (FCRR) continually evaluates reading programs. Their Web site is located in the back of this book, along with many other resources. Many schools purchase programs to teach reading. New programs are continually being developed. Even when programs are purchased, intervention teams may find that they need additional research-based interventions. The interventions in this chapter are research-based and can be used independently or as a supplement to other reading programs when students are not responding to those programs.

READING INTERVENTIONS

Reading is an essential skill for not only succeeding in school, but for succeeding in life. When students cannot read in elementary school, the problem is magnified as they go into secondary schools and cannot read their textbooks (Francis, Shaywitz, Steubing, Shaywitz, & Fletcher, 1996). It is far better to ease this problem during the elementary school years with effective interventions. Most struggling readers can be helped. They can succeed in learning to read (Foorman, Francis, Fletcher, Schatschneider, & Mehta, 1998). There are key ingredients for students to learn how to read (Snow, Burns, & Griffin, 1998).

Practice

Do you remember when you learned to drive a car? It felt like there was so much to learn. You had to think through everything you did, such as starting the car, shifting into drive, stepping on the gas, using turn signals, and braking. The more you did it, the less you had to think about it. It became a natural process. Practice helps students read better too (Snow et al., 1998).

Guided Practice

Guided practice is practicing what is learned. Teachers present the lesson and students practice doing the work, and then they receive feedback from their teachers.

Independent Practice

Independent practice is practice that students do independently. Teachers monitor the practice and provide support as needed.

Explicit Instruction

Students need explicit instruction in reading, especially in phonemic awareness and phonics (Snow et al., 1998). They learn best when teachers model and teach the skills they need. These skills need to be clearly taught (National Reading Panel, 2000). If students are left on their own to learn, they often make the same mistakes over and over again, and because they practice and repeat the mistakes, they learn them. This must be prevented. They need teacher support. The explicit instruction needs to be frequent. For students with severe reading difficulties, the intervention needs to be daily in two sixty-minute sessions over the course of six to nine weeks. A study of struggling readers was done using explicit instruction, and the students made dramatic gains that persisted for several years after the intervention was finished (Torgesen, 2001).

I have a friend who teaches first grade and is a master at using explicit instruction. Here are the steps she uses:

- Excite the students about what will be learned.
- Demonstrate the information to be learned.
- Have students practice.
- Provide support.
- Demonstrate again if needed.
- Have students practice some more.
- Provide support.

She starts the lesson with an introduction that is filled with enthusiasm and encouragement about what the students will be learning. When she teaches reading, she sounds the words out slowly and clearly. Then she has the students practice. If a student makes a mistake, she never tells them they are wrong. Instead, she says, "I will have a turn now." She then teaches them the sounds in a more dramatic, explicit way. She repeats this process until the students have learned the material.

Hands-On Materials

This same friend uses hands-on materials that students can manipulate as they learn to read. This is effective for the early grades as students practice in phonics and word identification (Pullen, Lane, Lloyd, Nowak, & Ryals, 2005). She uses sandpaper letters that students trace as they sound out the letters, a small movable alphabet for students to sound out and put words together, and cards students use to match objects to sounds. It becomes a game for the students to manipulate all the materials.

Systematic Sequential Instruction

The rule of thumb is to teach students reading beginning with the easier skills and then progress to more difficult skills. This is done in a systematic sequential manner (Snow et al., 1998). When students master one skill, they progress to the next skill so there are no gaps.

Differentiated Instruction

The only way to truly reach all learners and teach them to read or teach them any other skill is to do it in a differentiated manner that accommodates the needs of each individual learner (Foorman & Torgesen, 2001). In the differentiated classroom, there are some students working individually, some in small groups, some in larger groups, and some working with the teacher. Chapter 5 is devoted to how to differentiate. This is an important cornerstone for RTI.

Application Using Meaningful Text

Have you ever read words and had no idea what they meant? Students can learn to read, but if they do not understand the meaning of the words, they get nothing from what they are reading. They need to have word study vocabulary so they can learn and not guess the meaning of words.

LITERACY FOR ELEMENTARY SCHOOLS

Five Essential Components

There are five essential components for effective literacy in elementary schools: (1) phonemic awareness, (2) phonological processing, (3) fluency, (4) vocabulary, and (5) text comprehension (Denton, Vaughan, & Fletcher, 2003).

Phonemic Awareness

Spoken language is comprised of phonemes (individual sounds) put together to form words (Kemp & Eaton, 2008). Words each have meaning. Without the ability of phonemic awareness, the meaning of words can be lost. Phonemic awareness is the conscious awareness of the sounds in spoken words. Students need to learn phonemic awareness at an early age.

Make sure that lessons are fun and engaging (Vaughn & Roberts, 2007). Students learn with activities that include the following:

- Identifying objects in the environment by their beginning or ending sounds
- Rhyming words
- Clapping to the number of syllables
- Reading books aloud with emphasis on sounds
- Matching games with letters and objects
- Matching words to objects
- Identifying the location of phonemes in words, as in beginning, middle, or end of the words, and connecting phonemes to make words

Phonological Awareness

Phonological awareness is the awareness of the spoken language in all its forms: words, sentences, phrases, and phonemes (Kemp & Eaton, 2008). Phonemes are one component of phonological awareness, but separate because without the ability to understand the individual words, there can be no comprehension of phrases and sentences. This is something that is taught with activities similar to the ones for phonemic awareness, but on a more advanced level. Teach students how to chunk and read the different syllables in words (Vaughn & Roberts, 2007). Help them understand root words so they can more easily recognize unfamiliar words. Activities include the following:

- Listening activities
- More advanced rhyming activities
- Word awareness
- Syllable awareness
- Phonemic awareness activities

Fluency

Fluency is the ability to read with speed, expression, and accuracy. The fluent reader recognizes words easily, reads aloud effortlessly, and can then focus on comprehension. Fluent readers make the correct intonations and pauses as they read with expression. Students who are not fluent usually read slowly, haltingly, make frequent mistakes, and the feeling of the meaning behind the words is lost (Rasinski & Lenhart, 2008)

More Is Better

It takes practice to become a fluent reader. Teach fluency by having multiple activities involving meaningful reading (Jenkins, Zumeta, Dupree, & Johnson, 2005). The more that students are exposed to words, the more they will easily recognize the words and be able to read them rapidly, with the appropriate expression. Some strategies to increase fluency include the following:

- Books on tape
- Peers reading to struggling readers
- Adults reading to struggling readers (you can use volunteers)
- Choral reading in which students as a group read aloud together
- Echo reading in which the teacher reads a sentence with expression, and then the class as a group reads it with same expression
- Tape-assisted reading in which students read along with a story tape
- Students reading fun poems
- Reader's Theatre in which students perform a script based on meaningful literature

Vocabulary

Vocabulary is a key concept in literacy as well. Students who have limited vocabulary are handicapped in their ability to understand and to read. I was one of those students. English is my second language. When I started kindergarten, I did not understand a word the teacher or my class-mates said. There are other students like me who have English as their second language. I am fortunate in that when I went to school they were not looking for learning disabilities. If they had been, I may have been diagnosed because my lack of English vocabulary seriously impacted my ability to understand, to follow directions, and to read. Fortunately, I caught up with the other students. Not all students are that fortunate.

There are other students who start school with limited vocabularies not because English isn't spoken in the home, but because no one is doing much talking in their homes. Building vocabulary is easier when it is part of an environment where it is frequently used. That is how children learn to talk. That is where they grasp the rich meanings of the words they hear and say.

Begin with making sure that students know the most basic words like *school*, *mother*, *father*, and *home* (Kemp & Eaton, 2008). Take nothing for granted. When I started school, I did not know those basic words.

Students may be puzzled with even the most basic instructions. Next, ensure that students know words that are used frequently in your classroom. These can be words such as *instructions*, *directions*, and even the word *vocabulary*.

Text Comprehension

Students may be able to read something fluently, but it is another thing to be able to understand what they have read.

Story Grammar

When students read, they generally are most familiar with the regular narrative type of reading. This is where there is a sequence of events leading to an end with characters and actions (Reid & Lienemann, 2006). Students may need help in understanding the story. Have several questions that students see prior to reading the story, and can think about as they read (Mathes & Fuchs, 1997). The questions are about the characters and the story. Students identify the main character, the way the character felt, what the main character did, where the story takes place, and how the story ends.

Expository Text

Students are generally familiar with the types of stories that are narrative, but expository text is different. It is not a story; instead, it is information. Students have to learn how to decipher the information.

Making Up Questions

One of the ways students can think more about what they read is to involve them in coming up with their own questions while they are reading (Davey & McBride, as cited in Reid & Lienemann, 2006). This helps them be more involved and focused on the important concepts they are reading.

Graphic Organizers

This is a method for students to take the information they are reading and put it into a graphic. The graphic helps them better understand what they are reading. The Key Points to Remember chart shown in Figure 3.1 is an example of a graphic organizer. When giving directions to students for the Key Points chart, have them do the first paragraph of the story, a middle paragraph, and the last paragraph. Another option is to have them do three paragraphs in the body of the story.

Figure 3.1 Key Points to Remember

Name _____ Date _____

Text _____

Paragraph 1 Key Point	Paragraph 2 Key Point	Paragraph 3 Key Point
Supporting Facts	**Supporting Facts**	**Supporting Facts**

Figure 3.2 Story Map

Name _____ Date _____

Text _____

Characters

Setting

Time

Problem

Actions

Ending

Story Map

The Story Map is a graphic organizer designed to improve reading comprehension (Daqi, 2007). It helps students stay focused on the different aspects of the story to improve their comprehension by identifying key parts of the story (see Figure 3.2).

LITERACY FOR SECONDARY SCHOOLS

Students with poor literacy skills enter secondary schools at a real disadvantage. They need to be proficient in literacy for content mastery in the different subjects. There is hope. Many years ago I met a man, John Corcoran, who had not been able to read in school. He said his problems began when he started elementary school. Other students all started reading, but he could not. He said he had to keep it a secret, and that he was profoundly embarrassed and ashamed because he knew that he was different from everyone else. He passed through the primary and secondary grades and received an athletic scholarship for college. He somehow completed college and graduated with a teaching certificate. He still could not read. He got a job as a teacher. He was always on guard that someone would find out his secret. Finally, he quit. He married a wonderful woman and shared his secret with her. He started a company as a building contractor, and she did all of his reading for him. He was extremely successful, and it gave him the confidence he needed to one day go into a literacy center, walk up to the woman there, and say, "I can't read. Will you help me?" And that is when his life changed dramatically. That was the beginning of a new life for him. He was interviewed on television shows, and he went to the White House. Former First Lady Barbara Bush asked him to help fight against illiteracy. He served on the national literacy board and today has a national foundation called the John Corcoran Foundation to help others who cannot read. John Corcoran learned how to read as an adult. He learned, and so too can secondary students.

Literacy is very important in secondary schools. Teachers are under pressure to have students meet state standards in content areas. If students cannot read, they cannot pass standardized tests. Teachers have more students to teach daily, and this amplifies the pressure. Instead of one class of twenty to thirty-five students, the secondary teacher may teach one hundred fifty students in a day. In addition to Tier 1 interventions, some secondary schools implement reading labs to help students, as well as before- and afterschool reading programs. Some schools have tutorials offered by teachers within the classrooms to supplement instruction.

Tier 1 instruction can still be in the general education classroom. In an ideal world, every class would have a co-teacher, and the teachers would divide their roles and responsibilities so that struggling readers can be taught. However, this is costly, and will not occur in the majority of schools. Instead, secondary teachers need to differentiate instruction in order to help students with varying abilities. Some students can then work in small groups, others can work independently, and still others can work in larger groups.

There are strategies that have been found to be effective for teaching struggling readers. These are all strategies that can be used for either Tier 1 or Tier 2.

Collaborative Strategic Reading

This is a method of motivating, engaging, and helping struggling readers learn. It consists of four strategic reading comprehension strategies (Vaughn & Klingner, 1999).

Preview

The preview is designed to motivate students about what they are going read. It often reminds them of background knowledge, and they learn to make predictions about the text. Students take several minutes to preview the text and search for information to help them make predictions. As they do this, they become familiar with vocabulary related to the text. They then take several minutes to have a group discussion about the preview. They also discuss what they want to learn from reading the text.

Click and Clunk

Students identify parts of the text that are difficult. It can be described to students that sometimes when they meet someone, they "click." They instantly feel a connection. Students are asked to identify parts of the text that "clicks" for them. A "clunk" is explained as something that feels like you are running into a brick wall. Students are asked to identify the "clunks," or the things that are difficult for them. Students fix their clunks by reading the sentences with clunks and looking for clues; reading sentences with clunks, but leaving out the word that is the clunk and then trying to figure out what the clunk was; looking for prefixes or suffixes in the words that are clunks; and asking for help.

Get the Gist

Students look for the "gist," or the main idea of different passages within the text. They find the main idea and rephrase it in their own words in a sentence.

Wrap-Up

The students review what they read. They ask and answer questions about the reading that helps them remember what they read.

Strategic Instruction Model

This is a method to help students think critically about what they have read. It gives them specific strategies and skills to help them learn (Hock & Mellard, 2005). Some of those strategies include the following:

- Paraphrasing
- Learning to express the ideas in their own words
- Self-questioning
- Developing their own questions about reading passages and then finding the answers to those questions
- Visualizing scenes in the text in detail

Computer-Assisted Instruction (CAI)

Computers are the way of the future, and in many schools, the future is here. There are many students showing significant gains in learning using computers (Moore, 1988). The gains are magnified when teachers are involved as tutors for students, cheering them on to success. The key is to find appropriate software and to supervise the students (Snow, 2005).

SUPPLEMENTAL INTERVENTIONS FOR EITHER ELEMENTARY OR SECONDARY OR BOTH

The following interventions are not research-based, but they have been used successfully with students by me and many others.

Letter Reversals

Attach a visual strip to the student's desk or notebook so there is a model of the symbols that are typically reversed. Remind students to look at the letters as they write.

Loses Place, Omits Words, Skips Lines

Word Windows

Word windows are rectangular, small sheets with a transparent opening in the center (Appelbaum, 2008). Students put the word window over the page they are reading, and it helps them read one line at a time so they can keep their place while reading.

Bookmarks

Students follow their place using a bookmark. The bookmarks need to be plain so they are not distracting to students. Make them yourself out of card stock that is then laminated.

Adapt Worksheets

Teach students how to adapt their worksheets. For example, have students cover their worksheets with a blank sheet of paper so they do only one question at a time.

Copies

Take important materials that students need to read and make copies of the most important pages. Students can underline important items as they read.

E-Books

There are some students who have a difficult time reading regular books, but they do well with e-books.

Recorded Books

For students who have difficulty reading, get pre-recorded books. Many students have their own iPods, or you can get books on tape. These may be students who are auditory learners rather than visual learners, and they may thrive with the recorded books.

Tracing With Highlighter

You can find erasable highlighters at office supply stores. Students highlight important information in their texts and then later erase the highlighter.

Tracing With Fingers

Students trace each line as they read with their fingers. It helps them keep their place on the page.

Check Beginning Three Letters

Students frequently guess at words as they read. Teach them to look at the first three letters of words that are difficult before they say the word (Appelbaum, 2008).

Colored Overlays

This is a remarkable and simple strategy that can help students with reading fluency (Wilkins, 2002). I have heard over and over again from teachers as I travel across the country speaking about how effective it has been for their students. The overlays come in different colors. They are large, transparent, colored sheets of paper. Students choose a color that is most effective for them, put it over the reading material, and then they read (Appelbaum, 2008). That's it! It's so simple and yet so effective. I have found that different students do better with different colors of transparent sheets. I went to a scrapbooking store and bought inexpensive sheets in a variety of colors. One teacher told me she had used the sheets, and one of her students was so dependent on them she asked the student's family to buy him a pair of glasses with that color lenses. It worked!

Difficulty Copying Correctly

Correct Vision

When students have problems copying they may have vision problems. Be alert to see if students have problems visually. They may squint and avoid close or far work depending on the vision problem.

Note Taker

Assign a student who takes excellent notes to be an anonymous note taker. Give note takers carbonless paper for taking notes. At the end of the class, note takers hand you their extra set of notes, and you give them to the students with learning disabilities.

Easily Distracted

Sit students who are easily distracted away from noise and sights that are distracting.

Air Vents

Air vents can be so distracting that students do not hear you or anything else in the classroom. They only hear the "whirring" of the heater or air conditioner. Seat students who are easily distracted away from vents.

Open Doors and Windows

Have you ever been in a room with the television set turned on? It's hard to resist watching it. It's the same for students who sit near open doorways looking into the hall or windows looking outside. Make sure students who are easily distracted are sitting in seats positioned to minimize distractions.

Study Carrels

One way to stop distractions is to have students use study carrels. I make my own out of file folders and call them private offices (Appelbaum, 2008). Take two file folders and slide them together so that the left flap of the first one is on the outside, and the right side becomes the back of the private office. The second folder has its right flap open on the right, and its left side is also the back of the office. Glue them together, and then laminate them. Give all students their own private offices.

Highlight Key Points

Highlight key words on worksheets or instructions. Highlight words in the directions so that students better understand what to do, and highlight key words throughout the assignment.

Memory Deficits

Have you ever taught a student something, and it took a long, long time? The student finally mastered it, and you were both so pleased. Then the next day, the student comes to class and has forgotten it. Both you and the student are frustrated, but the student has a feeling you do not have— it's total embarrassment. The student may cover it up with a joke, but inside the student feels ashamed. Now imagine that this happens over and over again to the same student. There are some tricks you can use to help students remember better.

Use Mnemonic Devices

Mnemonics are aids to help memory (Harwell, 2001). They are little tricks that remind students of something they need to remember. They are associations that jog the mind. For example, "Thirty days hath September" is a mnemonic to help remember how many days there are in a particular month. You and the students make up your own mnemonics when students need to learn something new. Just like you have to practice "Thirty days hath September," so too will students need to practice the mnemonic when learning something new.

Seat Student Carefully

Because it is so easy to get distracted, it is important to seat students carefully.

Seat Near Teacher

Students sometimes like to "hide out" at the back of the room. Make sure to seat the students in the front of the room near you. This prevents distractions, and it gives you opportunities to monitor and reinforce appropriate behavior.

Seat Near Student Role Model

Seat students who need extra help near students who are role models. They can work cooperatively together, and students who need that extra help can learn from their peers.

Discover Keys to Student Success

You will be using progress monitoring and learning a lot about your students. Add to the information that you acquire. Design a questionnaire that tells you about students and their reading habits (see Figure 3.3, My Reading Favorites).

Figure 3.3 My Reading Favorites

Name _____ Date _____

Directions: Place a check in the spaces below next to your favorites.

__ Jokes	__ Animals	__ People
__ Picture Books	__ Magazines	__ Science
__ Sports	__ How Things Work	__ Poems
__ Real-Life Stories	__ Scary Things	__ Novels
__ Poems	__ Songs	__ Cars

Is reading fun for you? ___ Yes___ No ___ Sometimes

Do you have a favorite author? ___ Yes ___ No

If yes, who is your favorite author? _____

Why? _____

_____

_____

_____

_____

_____

What is your favorite book? _____

If you could receive any book as a gift, what book would it be? _____

_____

_____

_____

Do you ever read magazines or comics? If so, which ones?_____

_____

_____

_____

_____

MATH AND RTI

While literacy is important, math is too. Some people think math is simply about counting, but it is so much more. It is a language of its own—a language of symbols that describes the relationship between objects, events, and times (Fore, Boon, Laweson, & Martin, 2007). As technology becomes more and more important, it will increase the need for more mathematical thinking (Burns, 2005). Thus, research-based interventions for math will become more and more important.

Although more and more math programs are becoming available for both elementary and secondary schools, there was minimal research available at the time this book was written. There are resources that evaluate the different programs currently available listed in the back of this book, and as research becomes available, you will find more and more. One excellent source listed in the back of the book is the RTI Action Network, found at http://rtinetwork.org/.

I have listed some of the currently available research-based interventions below. The same three-tier model applies for mathematics as in the other subject areas. The interventions described can be used primarily for Tier 1 and Tier 2, depending on student needs.

Increased Drill and Practice

Just like practice is so important in literacy, it is also important in math. It is an effective method to improve learning (Woodward, 2006). Students need many opportunities to practice math.

Drill Sandwich

This involves having students practice math using half known items and half unknown items (Burns, 2005). It makes it easier for student than having them practice with all unknown items.

Incremental Rehearsal

Drills and practice begin with easier items so that students are more comfortable, and then they gradually move more and more to new items.

Manipulatives

Manipulatives help improve the learning of math (Donabella & Rule, 2008). One interesting study demonstrated that students who had previously scored low on state tests in mathematics learned multiplication better when they used a manipulative Montessori Checkerboard for Multiplication and other multiplication manipulatives. Not only did they learn better, but they also enjoyed the work and had more confidence in their mathematical abilities.

SUMMING IT UP

There are many research-based interventions for literacy, but there is very little research for math research-based interventions. As RTI becomes more established, there will be more and more research available because of the requirement for research-based interventions. Many of the interventions used in this chapter for literacy can also help with math. These include the following:

- Systematic sequential instruction
- Differentiated instruction
- Explicit instruction
- Guided practice
- Independent practice
- Making up questions

The next chapter contains academic interventions that can be used for teaching math as well as literacy and other subject areas.

Academic Interventions to Improve Learning in All Subject Areas

4

Believe in each student. It is a gift you give them.

—Maryln Appelbaum

Academic programs that enhance all subject areas can be improved using research-based interventions. These are interventions that help students focus, relax, and become motivated and involved in their learning. Some are fun for students. They are all designed to make students more successful. They are predominantly Tier 1 or Tier 2 interventions, depending on the student and the situation; however, in some cases they could be used for Tier 3 instruction. Some are more appropriate for elementary students and others can be used for both elementary and secondary students.

ACADEMIC INTERVENTIONS

Set Learning Goals

When students set their own goals for academic achievement, they are more likely to follow them (Konrad, Fowler, Walker, Test, & Wood, 2007). It is a form of self-determination that fosters strength and follow-through in students. Teach them to set goals. I have seen schools where students set a goal for themselves for the day at the beginning of each school day, and it was very effective.

Relaxation Training

There are students who have such high levels of anxiety that it has a negative impact on their learning (Cheek, Bradley, Reynolds, & Coy, 2002). I remember my own undergraduate school days. I would study for exams with a friend. We both knew the material equally well, but when we took the tests, my friend would freeze up. The result was that she had poor grades on her exams and got lower grades in her course work. In those days we did not know about the research on test anxiety or that there were ways to counter it. There are effective ways to teach students to relax.

Muscle Tensing and Relaxing

Have students tighten the muscles in their feet, then relax them (Serok, 1991). Next, they tighten the muscles in their ankles and relax them. They very slowly work up their entire bodies, tightening and then relaxing their muscles. When they get to their faces, they tighten their jaws and relax, then their cheek muscles and relax. They tighten their eyes, their foreheads, and the top of their heads. By the time they do the top of their heads, they generally feel very relaxed.

Visualization

Students benefit from being taught to relax (Cai, 2000). Teach them to visualize. Have them imagine they are in a peaceful setting. This is effective for students with anxiety.

Poised Self-Portrait

When students are feeling stressed, have them take out a blank sheet of paper and draw themselves being calm. They keep this sheet of paper out when they are taking tests or having to do seatwork that could produce stress. When they look at the self-portrait, their anxiety can decrease (Cheek et al., 2002).

Stop, Drop, and Roll

Researchers have found the "stop, drop, and roll" strategy to be effective for test anxiety (Cheek et al., 2002). When students are taking a test and start to feel anxious, they put their pencils or pens down and stop. They take their hands and lay them on the surface of their desks, then drop their heads down into a comfortable position. Once relaxed, they gently roll their heads while taking in and exhaling three deep breaths. When they are finished, they sit back up and start working on their tests again.

Jigsaw

The jigsaw technique is a cooperative learning strategy that is effective in helping students learn and apply academic content (Eppler & Huber, as cited by Glasgow & Hicks, 2003). It helps improve reading, thinking through facts, and summarizing facts. To use this technique, divide the class into five groups. Appoint a leader for each group. All students in the group have their own individual assignments about an aspect of the subject they are learning. For example, if they are studying the life of George Washington, one student is assigned to read about his role as a commander during the war. Another student is assigned to read about his childhood, while another student is assigned to learn about his key accomplishments as president. The students each study and read all they can about their individual assignment. They then leave their home groups and meet with students from the other groups who have the same assignment. They tell what they have found, compare notes, and each becomes even more of an "expert" on their particular part of the assignment. The students then go back to their original groups, and they each share their expertise. At the conclusion of the sharing, there is a test.

You can see how this could be a fun way for students to study in-depth about an assignment. It breaks it into segments so they are not overwhelmed by what they have to learn.

Attribution Training

What students say to themselves about their learning affects how they learn (Siegel Robertson, 2000). When students feel they cannot learn, they say to themselves, "I cannot learn." This creates a feeling of helplessness that has even more of an adverse affect on learning. This becomes part of the students' belief systems. The more they think they cannot succeed, the more they cannot succeed. They think if they do succeed, it is pure luck. The goal of attribution training is to teach them new ways to look at themselves and their learning situation.

Academic Positive Self-Talk Statements

There are ways to help students retrain their brains to think more positively about learning and their own abilities. Teach them new statements they can say to themselves. I like to have a list of positive academic self-talk statements (see Figure 4.1). I have students choose one self-talk statement they will focus on at the beginning of each class day. They write it on an index card that is left on their desks and look at it at least ten times each hour. They check off every time they look at it and read it to themselves (see Figure 4.2).

Figure 4.1 Positive Self-Talk Statements

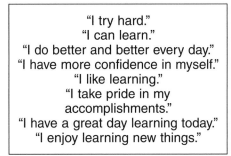

"I try hard."
"I can learn."
"I do better and better every day."
"I have more confidence in myself."
"I like learning."
"I take pride in my
accomplishments."
"I have a great day learning today."
"I enjoy learning new things."

Figure 4.2 Example of Positive Academic Self-Talk Check-Off Statements

I enjoy learning new things.

✓
✓
✓
✓
✓
✓
✓

Erase "Impossible"

There are other ways to teach students to say positive statements. One of my favorites is to have them take the classroom dictionary and find the word "impossible." Have them cross it out and write "possible" over it. Have them think of all of the things people thought were impossible that have been achieved. Talk about the cure for polio, or inventing an electric light, an automobile, or a telephone. All of these were things people at one time thought were impossible. Encourage students to not get stuck by what they or others may think is impossible.

Teacher-Student Relationship Quality

The research shows something that I believe with my whole heart, and that is student achievement is affected by relationships with teachers

(Hughes, Wen, Oi-Man, & Loyd, 2008). Students who have warm and supportive teachers and low levels of conflict achieve more (Connell & Wellborn, 1991). For me, the relationship between teachers and their students is the magic ingredient that can transform the academic lives of the students, and perhaps even affect them for their entire lives. I have seen this over and over again, not only when I taught and was an administrator, but also as a consultant to schools.

The reason this is so effective is because students who have warm and accepting relationships with their teachers are more motivated to follow classroom rules and are more accepting of their teacher's expectations. This converts to gains in student achievement.

Teacher Effort

What are the ingredients for successfully engaging students? One key factor is for teachers to exert effort—to try hard and not give up when times get tough (Rothbart & Ahadi, as cited by Hughes et al., 2008). I have often said, "If a teacher gives up on students, the students give up on themselves." I believe all students need someone to believe in them, someone to see something in them that they may not see for themselves. When teachers exert an effort with students, they feel that someone cares about them and wants them to succeed. This can have a positive impact not only on their achievement, but also on their relationships with peers and others in the school.

Capture Student Attention

Another very important ingredient is that teachers must engage students by capturing their attention (Hughes et al., 2008). Students cannot learn if they are not paying attention to what the teacher is saying or assigning. They will be like ships floundering in the sea without a compass, going this way and that way, but not knowing where they really need to go.

Some key ingredients I have found to be helpful in establishing warm teacher-student relationships include the following:

- Smile at them.
- Greet them warmly when they enter the classroom.
- Acknowledge their strengths.
- Involve them in decision making.
- Be consistent.
- Have fun—your own enthusiasm is contagious.

Highly Preferred Academic Activities

I discuss highly preferred activities as a means for stopping inappropriate behavior, but it is also a tool to help students learn. Highly preferred activities are activities that hold the attention of students (Cipani, 1993). When the task is something they enjoy, they are more likely to be engaged. For example, Courtney had a hard time learning her multiplication tables. Her teacher, Ms. Simmons, gave her some concrete materials that she found at a teacher's workshop. Courtney was hooked. She could now see and feel what the different multiples looked like and she learned them.

Provide Choices

There are several methods for providing students with a choice (Kern et al., 1998). One method is to provide a choice in the order of the tasks they need to do. For example, there are three tasks that need to be completed within a certain time frame. List all three tasks, and as students complete them, they scratch them off. You choose the tasks, but they get to choose the order in which they do them. You can see how this is also effective for academic learning.

Allow students to have a choice in the materials they use. An example is to have unusual pencils and pens for them to use for their writing assignments. The fact that they get to choose which materials they will use for an assignment that may be uncomfortable somehow changes the entire mood of the assignment for them so it is now more fun.

Meaningful Learning

The more meaningful learning is to students, the more likely they are to listen and learn (Dunlap, Kern, & Worchester, 2001). Find ways to make the curriculum meaningful and come alive.

Momentum

Establish momentum so that when students begin a task, they will want to complete the task. Do this by giving a series of easy tasks first so the momentum builds, and then present the more difficult task (Horner, Day, Sprague, O'Brien, & Heathfield, 1991). You can do this on worksheets and homework assignments as well as quizzes. Start with what is easy so students have a sense of accomplishment and a feeling of "I can do this," then progress to the more difficult problems.

Modify Assignments

Students often procrastinate when doing assignments and then wait so long that they do not do them at all (Ferrari, 1994). There are modifications you can make to assignments so students want to do them (Paden & Stell, 1997).

Student-Set Assignment Deadlines

Have students set deadlines for assignment. This helps them to not drag their feet and get the job done. Research shows that if students choose their own deadlines, they miss fewer deadlines and accelerate the speed in which they do assignments (Roberts & Semb, 1989).

Modify Assignment Difficulty

When students feel a task is too difficult, they may feel so overwhelmed they do not even try to do a good job (Puffer, as cited by Paden & Stell, 1997). It can even be the antecedent for inappropriate behavior (Dunlap, Kern-Dunlap, Clark, & Robbins, 1991).

Break Learning Into Smaller Chunks

If an assignment is complex, break it into smaller chunks (Bodie, Powers, & Fitch-Hauser, 2006). When students complete one chunk, they get to go on to the next chunk. Now, instead of an assignment being too difficult, it becomes more fun to complete one problem so that you can get to the next one.

I have a great way of helping students with this. Take an ordinary cream-colored office file folder, the type you use for filing papers. Open it so the entire file folder is in front of you. Take the flap on the left and divide it into three equal parts horizontally. Cut it so that the left flap now has three flaps. Put a sheet of paper with problems on the right hand side of the folder. Close the top left flap. You should now have three separate parts of the top part of your folder. Number the top flap "1," the middle flap "2," and the bottom flap "3." When students receive their worksheet, they put the sheet into their folder. They open the first flap, work those problems, and then close the flap. They then work the problems under the second flap, close it up when finished, and work on problems under the third flap. When they are finished, they open all three flaps to make sure they did not miss anything.

Modify Amount of Teaching—Less is More

It is better to teach less and teach it in more depth than to cover a broad range of information about a topic (Eylon & Linn, 1988). Too much information can make students feel overwhelmed and they "shut off."

Modify Method of Student Response

Some students need to have the method of response modified to make the task easier (Paden & Stell, 1997). There are students who cannot take multiple choice or true and false tests. However, these students do well on essay tests and shine as they express all the information they know. Observe and talk to students to discover ways to modify response modes so you still know they have completed the work.

Modify Assignment Appeal

Assignments need to be appealing to students so they want to do them (Paden & Stell, 1997). Create more excitement by giving students a chance to problem solve rather than just listening to lecture. Have students do projects in groups. Invite guest speakers. Do demonstrations. Allow students to use the Internet.

Modify Assignment Instructions

Make sure instructions for assignments are clear. Demonstrate the assignments so it is very clear what you want students to do. Have oral and written instructions. Use task cards with written instructions or write the instructions on the whiteboard for students so they not only hear the instructions from you, but they get to see them in writing.

Do a task checkup. After students have received instructions, have them pair up with a partner and take turns repeating the instructions to each other. It is a way of checking to see if they are on target. It is surprising how many times students have caught errors in their perceptions.

Vary Tasks

Intersperse more difficult tasks with easier tasks. An example of this can be found in a study done with math (Logan & Skinner, 1998). Students had problems completing assignments that involved multiplying double-digit numbers. When the instructor mixed the double digits in with easier single-digit multiplication, the students did better.

Employ Active Learning

Studies show students learn better using active learning techniques (Tanner & Roberts, 1996). Increase student involvement, and you will increase student motivation. The more motivated students are, the more they want to perform. Active learning means exactly what it says: students are more active and involved in their own learning. Student projects, debates, and problem solving all are methods for using active learning. You will learn many differentiated instruction strategies involving active learning in Chapter 5.

Use Hands-On Learning

Some students need more of a hands-on approach to learning. An interesting study was conducted in Nigeria that showed the effectiveness of manipulatives (Aburime, 2007). There were two groups of students who had difficulty with learning math. One group had teachers who cut geometric shapes out of paper and had students use the shapes to learn geometry. The other group learned geometry the regular way without manipulatives. The first group learned better with the manipulatives.

Employ Peer-Assisted Learning Strategies (PALS)

PALS is simply what the name implies: a peer-assisted learning strategy that has been proven to be effective in boosting student learning (McMaster, Shu-Hsuan Kung, Insoon, & Cao, 2008). The research on it has been effective in both reading and math (Fuchs, Fuchs, Mathes, & Simmons, 1997). Peer partners meet from two to five times a week for thirty- to forty-minute sessions, depending on the grade level and subject area. The student who needs the extra coaching practices an assignment for the student who is the coach. The coach gently corrects the student when needed. For example, Jordan needed help with reading. Kyle is his coach. Jordan reads two different passages from an assignment aloud to Kyle. Each reading is for one minute at a time. At the end of the minute, Jordan stops and receives feedback from Kyle. The feedback is always phrased in a positive way.

Coaches need to be carefully chosen to be a good fit for students who need help. Typically teachers use scores from tests to determine the pairings. The student pairs and the teacher choose target learning situations together. The coach may model the correct behavior. For example, a student may be having problems with multiplication. The coach models the correct way to do a problem and asks questions to guide the other student to success with the problem. When the student correctly works a problem, the coach circles the answer to show it is correct and praises the student. If the student makes a mistake, the coach gives additional help.

EMPLOY ASSESSMENT

Assessment can be a vehicle to improve learning. For example, in one study, a group of students took a pre-test and another group of students did not. When the first group of students took the test again, their scores were higher than the group that did not have the pre-test (Foos & Fisher, 1998). Testing can be very valuable for students when they learn to evaluate themselves so they can do better the next time.

Formative Assessment

Formative assessment is a form of feedback that can lead to student achievement (William, Lee, Harrison, & Black, 2004). It is not necessarily used for grading purposes, however. It is simply feedback to learn more about students and what they need. There are many ways to get student feedback, and determine what they know and what they still need to learn. This is a good tool to use in addition to progress monitoring.

Traffic Lights

Students have three round circles representing a traffic light on their desks. When they understand an answer, they have the green circle showing. When they are puzzled and unsure if they understand the answer, they have the yellow light showing. When they do not understand the lesson or assignment, they have the red circle facing the teacher.

Smiley Faces

Smiley faces are a similar concept to the traffic lights (Bambara & Kern, 2005). There are three types of large faces. When students understand the teacher, they have a smiley face on their desk so the teacher can see they understand. When they are puzzled, they have a face that looks puzzled facing the teacher. When they do not understand the assignment or lesson, they put a frown face on their desk.

Open-Ended Questions

Have conversations with students and ask them open-ended questions. You can do this one-on-one, in small groups, or as a whole class.

Which Road?

This is a fun game to introduce a new topic and get a quick idea of student knowledge. Point out four different corners in the classroom. Tell students that each corner represents a road. They are to go to the corner of the classroom that matches their knowledge about the new topic. One corner is the dirt road, meaning they know nothing about the topic. A second corner is a paved road, which means they know a little. The third corner is the highway, which means they know some information about the topic, and the last corner is the yellow brick road, which signifies that students are experts on the topic.

High Five

Ask students to hold up a number of fingers to signify how well they know different areas of a topic. They hold up their fingers on a scale with one being the lowest and five the highest.

Rotation Thinking

This is another fun game to find out what the entire classroom knows about a topic. Hang poster-sized charts around the classroom. Each one has a heading with a different aspect of the topic. Students go around the room adding what they know about the topic. A variation of this is to post sheets with the 5 W's. These are: Who, What, When, Where, and Why. Students walk around the room and fill in those sheets with what they know about the topic. You can also make this a worksheet for each student to do individually.

Three Key Points

After learning a concept, students write three key points about what they learned.

"Aha" Page

After learning a concept, students summarize what they learned on an "Aha page."

Role-Play

Students role-play something they have learned. A variation is to break the class into three groups, and each group role-plays another part of the targeted learning for each other.

Poem or Song

Students write a poem or song using five key points they have learned.

Scrapbook

Students create a scrapbook of what they have learned. It can be about any type of learning. They can even make a scrapbook of math facts.

Identifying Similarities and Differences

When students learn to identify the similarities and differences about a concept, they gain understanding of the topic (Stahl & Fairbanks, 1986).

REINFORCE EFFORTS

When students are reinforced for their efforts to learn something, their achievement increases (Van Overwalle & De Metsenaere, 1990). There are different ways you can reinforce students.

Student Self-Rating Reinforcement

Have a rating scale of zero to three that students use to rate their own efforts. Zero means they have exerted no effort. One means they have exerted a little effort. Two means they have exerted more effort. Three means they have exerted a lot of effort (see Figure 4.3). Rating them higher all the time can act as reinforcement for students to increase their efforts in learning (Van Overwalle & De Metsenaere, 1990).

Teacher Reinforcement

Verbal Recognition

I have found that many students hear what they do that is wrong, but few hear what they do that is correct. Take the time to tell students when they have done something correctly. Your words can be like sunshine to a plant. Just as sunshine helps a plant to thrive, your words of recognition and encouragement can help students thrive.

Figure 4.3 Student Self-Rating Chart

Date	Assignment	Effort

Tangible Reinforcement

There are some students for whom tangible rewards help them to complete their assignments (McLaughlin & Malaby, 1975). These students need a reward that they can see and experience, such as a sticker or an earned privilege.

Task Reinforcement

There are students who will work harder to earn the privilege of doing a task or a chore. Some of these tasks include taking something to the office, helping grade papers, and cutting up paper.

Cueing and Questions

Cueing and questions are key strategies to guide students in their learning (Marzano, Marzano, & Pickering, 2003). Use cueing and questions that help students focus on the key points they need to learn. Ask questions that require students to think and analyze information.

Exercise

Exercise boosts learning (Reynolds & Nicolson, 2007). It also reduces symptoms of inattention. One study by Reynolds and Nicolson showed that students who exercised also did better in motor skills, speech and language fluency, phonology, and working memory.

EXAMPLE OF THREE TIERS

Here is an example of how to incorporate these interventions into three tiers for a student who has difficulty focusing and paying attention. Patrice would often begin an assignment and then stop and doodle or stare into space. Universal screening showed that Patrice had no reading problems. The problem was with her classroom work. Figure 4.4 shows a possible intervention plan using only the interventions listed in this chapter. It is a hypothetical plan and, in reality, would be used along with other behavioral interventions to improve her learning academically.

Figure 4.4 Patrice: Hypothetical Example Using Three Tiers

Tier	Intervention(s)	Location	Time	Person	Duration
1	• Set learning goals daily • Modify assignment difficulty	General education classroom	30 minutes	General education teacher	2 times a week for 4 weeks
2	• Employ manipulatives • Build momentum	Outside of classroom	30 minutes	Interventionist	2 times a week for 8 weeks
3	• Attribution training • Cueing and questions	Outside of classroom	60 minutes	Interventionist	5 times a week for 8 weeks

Differentiating Instruction

5

Learning is a great adventure in which teachers and students embark together to explore new ideas and new worlds.

—Maryln Appelbaum

Response to Intervention requires responding to the needs of students with individualized interventions and progress monitoring. This is typically done within the general education classroom. How can a teacher teach a large group of students and still have time to help these students? Moreover, how can the general education teacher continually progress monitor students within the structure of the larger general education classroom? The answer is differentiating instruction. Differentiating instruction is adapting to the needs of the individual students.

WHAT THE RESEARCH SHOWS TO SUPPORT DIFFERENTIATED INSTRUCTION

When a teacher correctly matches the student's skill level with appropriate learning tasks, there is an increase in student achievement. (Fisher et al., 1980)

A longitudinal study showed that students whose skills were under-challenged demonstrated low involvement in learning activities and less concentration. (Csikszentmihalyi, Rathunde, & Whalen, 1993)

The best learning environment offers a large variety of choices to satisfy individual abilities and talents. (Jensen, 1998)

Research has shown that accommodating the learning style through appropriate teaching and counseling interventions results in significant academic and attitude gains. (Sullivan, 1993)

Differentiated instruction is a process in which teachers learn to change their pace, style, and level of instruction in response to student differences. These include different interests and different readiness levels (Fisher, 2008). They also include the different learning styles of students (Sullivan, 1993). There are three specific areas in which to differentiate: the content of the lesson, the process used to teach, and the final product.

Figure 5.1 Differentiate

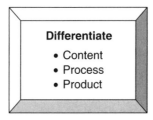

I have used differentiated instruction for many years, even before it was called differentiated instruction. I knew that I had to do something to reach the diverse needs of my students. I had students with cultural differences, students with different learning styles, students with different interests, students with disabilities, and students with varying backgrounds in learning. I had to find a way to meet the needs of all of these diverse learners in a large class. I observed differentiated instruction in action at another school on a professional day, and I thought, "That's it! This will work for my own students." It was a slow process. It is not something that a teacher or school can decide to implement the next day or even the next month. It requires different methods of teaching, and constant assessment of the students and yourself to check for progress. However, I can attest to the fact that it works! I found that the most effort required by me was in the initial years of implementation, and involved making and finding different lessons and materials to meet the curriculum and the needs of students. After the first few years, it was much easier. It will be easier for you too.

In this chapter you will learn some of the fundamental concepts for implementing differentiated instruction in your classrooms. Differentiating instruction, like implementing RTI, is a process. It requires professional development and time to implement. There are parts that can be implemented quickly, and others that involve setting up and creating materials that require more time. This chapter is designed to give you the basics to get started on the road to differentiation.

FLEXIBLE GROUPING

Flexible grouping is the process of using different groupings for instruction (Chapman, 1995). There are parts of the day when students work independently and parts of the day when they work in small groups. The groups should to be based on the needs and interests of students. Students can be in one group for one subject or activity and in another group for another subject or activity.

The groups need to have clear rules (Gregory & Chapman, 2002). They need to have direct instruction on how to work together as a group. Students need to understand their task, their assigned roles within the group, where they can meet as a group, time lines for completion of tasks, and rules about how loudly they can speak in their groups.

Groupings

Student-Led Common Interest Groups

These are a group of students that all share a common interest (Hoffman, 2002). Sometimes these groups are formed on their own within learning centers as students work together on a common interest. There are typically five or fewer students. The group size is limited by the amount of workspace. The students work together and ask for help from each other. Your job as their teacher is to monitor the group to make sure the interactions are positive in nature, and that leadership of the group is passed from student to student.

Student-Led Shared Task Groups

These are small groups of four or five students that you purposely set up to be heterogeneous in ability, gender, and age. All of the students work together on the same task (Hoffman, 2002). The tasks are designed to maximize the heterogeneity of the group.

Dyads—Buddies

These are groups that are formed on their own with or without your help (Hoffman, 2002). They come together to mentor or tutor each other, and to support each other in learning. They also come together to share a task. It makes it more interesting for students to work together with a buddy.

Some Appropriate Activities for Heterogeneous Grouping

There are many appropriate, interesting, and fun activities for students in heterogeneous groups. They can have open-ended discussions about any topic. For example, they can talk about current events. They can engage in activities that require analysis, critical thinking, and forming concepts. They can take a solution and generalize other solutions. You can see where this could be fun for the group.

Appropriate Activities for Homogeneous Grouping

Homogeneous groups can also engage in many interesting and fun activities. They can use drills to practice with each other and/or study together for a recall-type test. You can give them questions they have to answer to demonstrate comprehension about what they have been learning.

The Research on Grouping

Prior to flexible grouping, grouping was done according to ability. Students always knew when they were in a low- or high-ability group. The research shows that this method of grouping was actually detrimental to low-ability students (Mason, Schroeter, Combs, & Washington, 1992). Conversely, students who are high-ability have no decrease in achievement as the result of flexible grouping (Mason et al., as cited by Mills, 1998). Everyone wins.

TIERED ASSIGNMENTS

Tiered assignments are tiered lessons students do in heterogeneous groups (Northey, 2005). It is a way to match students by their learning styles and interests. All students in the class would have the same objectives, and the content needs to take the same amount of time for each group.

There are different ways to tier the assignments. They can be tiered by complexity with one group being the least complex, one group more complex, and one group the most complex. Mrs. Kendricks taught social studies in an inner-city school. There had been a shooting in a nearby school, and all the students were talking about it. She decided to tier lessons for groups by complexity. She assigned one group to discuss and make a list of the causes of violence in schools. This was the least complex assignment. She had another group write slogans for their school to prevent violence. This was more complex. The third group had the most complex assignment. They had to discuss and then write a list of ways to combat violence in their school and in society. They were all working on the same project, but all worked on different tiers.

Another way to tier assignments is by product. Here's an example of how to do this. Kinesthetic learners do a project that involves building something. Visual learners design posters as their project. Auditory learners listen to songs to find the best one to describe what they are learning.

It is important that tiering is invisible. All students need to be excited about their activities. The work cannot seem like it is more or less than the other groups, just that it is different. All groups are equally active.

How to Organize the Groups

Give each group a task card (Shulman, 1993). A task card can be an index card or a half-or full-sized sheet of paper. Color the cards to indicate the different groups. Laminate them and place them at each group's workstation. The cards have the group's directions written out for them. Be specific with your directions, but still allow them freedom to create their projects.

When you are planning a tiered lesson, be sure to keep in mind the knowledge or skill that you want students to learn. You also need to decide how you will assess the assignments (see Figure 5.2).

ANCHOR ACTIVITIES

When students are working more independently, they often finish at different times. Anchor activities are activities that you plan ahead for those times. They are free-time activities that keep the attention of students (Tomlinson, 2001).

Examples of anchor activities include the following:

- Reading a book
- Writing in journals
- Keeping learning logs
- Using graphic organizers
- Reviewing material
- Managing a portfolio
- Practicing assignments
- Learning math using manipulatives

Figure 5.2 Tiered Lesson

Concept or Skill to Be Mastered
Standard
Initiating Activity to Engage All Students
Materials Needed
Method of Tiering
Tier 1
Tier 2
Tier 3
Form of Assessment

FOCUS ACTIVITIES

Focus activities are activities that help students focus and pay attention (Gregory & Chapman, 2002). They are so interesting that students block out other distractions while doing them. Focus activities can be questions, challenges, or problems. They may require recalling prior learned information and applying it. They can even be journal entries. An example of a focus activity is to read a chapter for homework and sit with your study buddy and together find "feeling" words to better understand the main character. Another example is to take a page or a paragraph from a chapter and rewrite it, putting a friend in the story. Still another example is to write down three things to remember from the day's lessons (Gregory & Chapman, 2002).

USE LEARNING CONTRACTS

When I first started differentiating instruction, I needed a method for keeping track of student work—and so did they. I devised contracts for them. A contract is an individualized approach to improve student learning and behavior. The contract places the responsibility and the choice for learning and behavior on the student. Contracts lead to self-directed learning (Knowles, 1986). They help students understand what is expected, teach them to manage their time, and help them take ownership of what they will be learning (Gregory & Chapman, 2002).

The contract is an agreement prior to the student beginning a project or unit in which the resources, steps toward completion, and evaluation criteria are set up and agreed to by the teacher and student. This is an effective tool for students to learn time management because the contracts need to be completed by a certain date.

The Process

When I started using learning contracts, I met individually with students to explain the concept of contracts. What I typically said was, "Did you know your parents signed some type of contract when they moved into your home? They signed a paper agreeing to pay a certain amount of money, and in exchange, they get to live in your home. Whenever they use a credit card, it is because they have signed a contract agreeing to pay for something in exchange for using the card. In our classroom, I have a contract for you too. The contract will tell you the work you will do each day. It will help both of us keep track of your class work so you can always do

Figure 5.3 Contract

I, _____

                                will

_____

_____

_____

_____

_____

_____

_____

_____

_____

_____

_____

_____

_____

_____

_____

I will complete this contract by:

_____

Date signed _____

_____

Student Signature

Date completed _____

_____

Teacher's Signature

Figure 5.4 Weekly Contract

Name _____ Week of _____

Monday	Tuesday	Wednesday	Thursday	Friday
_____ Student Signature	_____ Student Signature	_____ Student Signature	_____ Student Signature	_____ Student Signature
_____ Teacher Signature	_____ Teacher Signature	_____ Teacher Signature	_____ Teacher Signature	_____ Teacher Signature

the best you can. We will work on what goes into the contract together." You can see that the goal was to explain the reasoning behind using contracts to foster cooperation, and to make the contract a fun "grown-up" type of agreement.

When using contracts, set mutually agreed upon deadlines for completion of the contract. Renegotiate the contract if it is not working. Get feedback from the student before writing the next contract. The more the student is involved, the more likely the student will be to adhere to the contract.

Start out simply with a contract for only one activity (see Figure 5.3). You can later expand this to a full day's activities and then to a week's activities (see Figure 5.4). Some teachers use reinforcers such as stickers for completion of the contract. I never found that this was necessary. Completing each contract seemed to be its own reinforcer for students.

CUBING

Cubing helps students think about a topic from six points of view (Gregory & Chapman, 2002). It is an activity that can be done individually, with partners, or as a tiered assignment. If it is a tiered assignment, use several differently colored cubes, one for each group, with each cube having different tasks. If students work in groups, they typically work individually and then share their findings with their group.

Figure 5.5 Cube

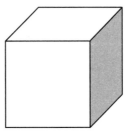

Cubes can be made out of any cube-shaped boxes. Cover them with construction paper. Each side of the cube has different directions (see Figure 5.6).

Figure 5.6 Cube Directions

Cube Side	Function	Verbs
One	Describe it	Name, locate, recall, list
Two	Compare it	Contrast, explain
Three	Associate it	Connect, make design
Four	Analyze it	Review, discuss, diagram
Five	Apply it	Suggest, propose
Six	Argue for it or against it	Debate, support

Cubing can be used for almost any subject area and for both elementary and secondary students. For example, students in Mr. Carson's class were studying the Holocaust. Several of the students were very passionate about the war because they had family members who perished in the Holocaust. They had heard their families talking about it. One student's great-grandfather was a Holocaust survivor who came in to speak to the class. Mr. Carson gave the students a cubing assignment on the Holocaust (see Figure 5.7).

You can see how this would be a lot of fun for students. They would all be working on the same project, but all at different levels.

Figure 5.7 Sample Cube Assignment: Holocaust

Side 1	Describe it	Describe the Holocaust.
Side 2	Compare it	Compare the Holocaust to the war in Iraq.
Side 3	Associate it	Compare Adolf Hitler to Saddam Hussein.
Side 4	Analyze it	Analyze World War II in relationship to the war in Iraq.
Side 5	Apply it	Apply how America now handles situations in which they see extermination of people.
Side 6	Argue for it or against it	Argue pro and con about world involvement helping people in countries where lives are in danger.

PROJECTS

A project is a form of investigating a topic that sparks the interests of students. As in the cubing example, it is a real-world topic (Chard, 1998). There are different ways to use project-based learning. It begins with the teacher selecting a topic for students to study based on student interests and curriculum standards.

The teacher discusses the topic with students and finds out what they already know about the topic. The more a subject sparks the interest of students, the better. Then the teacher helps students develop questions they will investigate for answers. It does not have to be a cubing project. It can be splitting the class into two or three groups, each working on different aspects of the topic. Students will need different resources to complete their projects, and the teacher helps them gather all of these resources. They may need different books, poster board, or even access to special sites on the Internet. There has to be a specific deadline for completion of projects to ensure that they do not go on for too long. The students also need monitoring to ensure they do not go off on a tangent and stop meeting the curriculum standard. There is usually an event that takes place where the students share their projects with the rest of the class and display the results (Curtis, 2002).

I have found that students are so engaged when they are working on projects that disruptive behavior is lessened. I also like projects because they allow students to work from their different learning styles. They are very motivational for students as they learn the subject matter in-depth in a very hands-on way.

A SPECIAL NOTE ABOUT DIFFERENTIATED INSTRUCTION

This chapter was intended to whet your appetite for differentiated instruction. It has a few of the basics you need to get started differentiating. Remember, differentiation is a process. Begin it slowly. It takes effort, but the results are rewarding. If you are the type of teacher that is used to having total control of your classroom, know that you are still going to be in charge, only in a different way. You are still the one to set the rules, to determine what will be studied and learned, to present the materials in an engaging way, and to assess the work. The difference now is that you will find you are more successful teaching all students. Differentiated instruction and Response to Intervention go hand-in-hand. Differentiated instruction will benefit all students. Your entire class will be learning in a way that excites them and has them excited about coming to school each day.

Be patient. Take it one step at a time, and slowly you will see your classroom transformed.

Positive Behavior Intervention and Support

6

A teacher's smile is worth riches to a struggling student.

—Maryln Appelbaum

Behavior management is an important key to success with Response to Intervention. If the students are not listening, they are not learning. There is no "one size fits all" type of strategy for behavior management. There is no single strategy that will fit every student in a school and help each of those students succeed. Moreover, there is no single strategy that will feel comfortable for every teacher. That is why when I speak or write, I believe very strongly in giving multiple strategies. RTI calls for continuous progress monitoring and adjusting. Teachers get to see exactly what will work with individual students. They get to modify and adjust. Even though the intent of the law behind RTI was originally to find and help students with learning disabilities (LD), now all students can be helped. In the past it was possible for students to do poorly for a variety of reasons other than LD. Those students fell through the cracks. I have seen students who were gifted, yet they were doing poorly because they were so bored. I have seen other students for whom English was a second language do poorly. There are students who have sensory issues, students with attention-deficit/hyperactivity disorder (ADHD), and students going through a tough time at home. There are many reasons students could be misbehaving or not learning. Now, these students will also be helped.

In addition to the interventions you will be learning, there need to be school-wide rules. These provide structure for all students, as well as the teachers, so that everyone in the entire school is on the same page.

POSITIVE BEHAVIOR INTERVENTION AND SUPPORT (PBIS)

PBIS is a comprehensive problem-solving method for designing comprehensive interventions for students (Bambara & Kern, 2005). This powerful method is not concerned with just the short-term goal of stopping inappropriate behaviors, but has a long-term goal of impacting the student's life and behavior in positive ways. It is a way of teaching students new, appropriate behaviors and changing the learning environment so they learn best. It has its foundation in four influences.

1. Applied Behavior Analysis

I first got involved in applied behavior analysis in undergraduate school when I had the opportunity to work in a residential treatment program and see first-hand how well it worked. Later I used it in my teaching career with students with disabilities. It is a systematic way of instruction that is extremely useful for teaching self-management skills (King-Sears & Carpenter, 1997). It is also effective for teaching students problem-solving skills (Dunlap et al., 2001).

2. Person-Centered Planning (PCP)

PCP emphasizes the importance of the individual student. It focuses the planning of interventions on the needs of individual students, rather than using interventions that apply to the entire class (Bambara & Kern, 2005). It is a method of valuing people, putting them first, and thinking of each person as an individual rather than as a disability. I remember when people used to say "ADHD students" rather than "students with ADHD." The former way put the disorder before the person. Now, it is the person that comes first and foremost. The emphasis is on the uniqueness of each person and their gifts rather than their deficits.

3. Self-Determination

This is the process of empowering students (Bambara & Kern, 2005). It means listening to the preferences and interests of students so they can be offered choices. Students learn how to make choices so they have more control over their own lives.

4. Inclusion

Inclusion involves the full participation of students in the general education classroom. Accommodations for students with disabilities are made in the general education classroom rather than sending students out to segregated classrooms or schools.

THE INTERVENTION PROCESS

An intervention entails coming up with a detailed, research-based, written plan of action to take care of a problem (McCook, 2006). This written plan needs to include the problem behavior. That may sound silly because most teachers think they already know the problem. However, I have found that when I speak to teachers, they generally say something like, "Jason is negative," "Tomas has a bad attitude," or "Kaitlin hates school." Those statements do not define the problem. They are "feelings." Instead, the inappropriate behavior needs to be concretely defined (Bambara & Kern, 2005). Here's an example: "Samuel gets up from his seat during seatwork and leaves the classroom without permission."

Step 1: Define the Problem Behavior

Destructive Behavior

There are generally three different types of problem behaviors. The first is destructive behavior. This is behavior that is harmful to the student or to others. This takes top priority over other problem behaviors because it can be life threatening.

Disruptive Behavior

Disruptive behaviors are those that interfere with learning and/or social relationships. They can include behaviors such as crying or refusing to do seatwork. Crying can interfere with other children wanting to socialize with the child. Refusing to do seatwork disrupts the learning process. Disruptive behaviors can escalate into destructive behaviors.

Distracting Behavior

George was a student who flapped his hands repeatedly. It made it difficult for other children to concentrate. It also made it difficult for George to do his own class work. Alex also had a distracting behavior. He tapped his pen or pencil on his desk. The noise distracted not only the other children, but his teacher as well. These are both examples of distracting behaviors.

Step 2: The Functional Assessment

This is a very important step in the positive behavioral support process (Bambara & Kern, 2005). Before you can design an intervention, you need to know why the behavior is occurring. You need to know if there is something going on in the classroom or at home that is creating the problem behavior. It means being a detective trying to figure out all you can about the student.

I was asked to consult in a school to help the teachers with students with behavior problems. I observed Mrs. Sachs teaching in her classroom. Casey was her problem student. When I spoke to Mrs. Sachs before the observation, she told me that he was disruptive, and it was totally wrecking her classroom. I asked her to define his behavior more clearly. She said that she liked to involve students in lively discussions, and he continually blurted out answers so that no one else got a chance to talk. I observed that Mrs. Sachs asked the students lots of questions to stimulate interest. Every time she asked a question, students would raise their hand. Casey did not raise his hand. He simply blurted out responses to each of her questions. Each time he would blurt out, she responded to him.

As I observed Casey, I used a key model for functional assessment called the "ABC Strategy." The letter A stands for antecedent. The antecedent is the event that occurs before the behavior. Some people call it the setting event because it sets the tone for the behavior to occur (Umbreit, Ferro, Liaupsin, & Lane, 2007). The antecedent in this case was Mrs. Sachs asking a question.

The letter B stands for behavior. In this case, the behavior was Casey blurting out. Mrs. Sachs would ask a question, and Casey would blurt out an answer every time.

The letter C stands for the consequence. The consequence is what occurs immediately following the behavior. The consequence causes the behavior to occur again. The consequence for Casey was that Mrs. Sachs responded to his blurting out. That was good news for Casey, so he kept doing it again and again. It was bad news for Mrs. Sachs, as her class was continuously disrupted.

Once I realized what was happening, I simply told Mrs. Sachs to stop calling on him when he blurted out. I told her to tell Casey ahead of time that the only way she would call on him would be if he raised his hand. I also had her give him a signal when he blurted out that served as a reminder if he forgot to raise his hand. Mrs. Sachs reported back that this was very effective with Casey.

When I am observing a child, I collect written data. I keep a running account of the times disruptive behavior happens. Each time the disruptive behavior occurs, I record it, the time it occurred, what I perceive to be the antecedent, and the consequence. I also include my initials for each behavior. I do this because I may ask the teacher to take over doing the recording, and each person may perceive an event differently. When teachers use a form like this, they may be co-teaching and someone else in the room may help them with the collection of the data. See Figure 6.1 for an example.

I intentionally described a simpler situation. Not all problem behaviors are this easily solved. The antecedent may be something that is occurring at home. I have seen cases in which students were behaving appropriately, but suddenly their behavior changed, even though nothing in the classroom has changed. Jay was one of those students. He was a dark-haired, tall, slim boy. He had many friends and did his class work appropriately. Then suddenly, it seemed like overnight, this all changed. Jay had difficulty paying attention and got up from his seat frequently. He started pushing and shoving his friends and using inappropriate language. Everything in the classroom was the same. When I spoke to his mother, she told me that Jay's dad had left, and they had no idea where he was. She was very angry and spoke harshly about her husband. The antecedent behavior in this case was the dad leaving and the total disruption of Jay's home life.

You can see how important it is to collect data like this prior to having an intervention. If a person comes to a doctor with horrible abdominal cramps, and the doctor merely treats the symptoms with an over-the-counter stomach medication, this may or may not cure the problem. The patient may have cancer, appendicitis, an abdominal virus, or another illness. To accurately treat the patient, the doctor has to play the part of a "detective" looking at all the symptoms to determine accurately what is causing the cramping. Then the doctor will know what to do to treat the patient. That is what you have to do with students too. You have to look at what was occurring prior to the behavior, look at the behavior, and then look at what occurs as a result of the behavior.

Figure 6.1 Example of ABC Chart

Time	A—Antecedent	B—Behavior	C—Consequence	Observer Initials
9:03	Teacher asks question	Student blurts out answer	Teacher answers	MA
9:05	Teacher asks question	Student blurts out answer	Teacher answers	MA
9:08	Teacher asks question	Student blurts out answer	Teacher answers	MA
9:13	Teacher asks question	Student blurts out answer	Teacher answers	MA

There has been functional behavior analysis research on changing antecedent conditions and how this can affect behavior (Kern, Choutka, & Sokol, 2002). This is good news for education. This means there is evidence that changing the antecedent can change the behavior in positive ways. These studies showed antecedent conditions set up circumstances for problem behaviors to occur. These antecedent conditions included academic tasks that were too difficult in which there was lack of student interest. They also included classroom environmental factors such as being too far from the teacher, a change in the schedule without any warning, and wait times when students became bored. Interestingly, it also showed physiological conditions such as hunger and fatigue. When these antecedent conditions were modified, the problem behaviors stopped.

Many times the students you will be observing may be in your own classroom. It is important to stay impartial when you are observing them. I have had teachers ask me, "How many times do I have to observe the student before I understand what is happening?" My answer is that when I first started observing students using the ABC model, I observed for several days to a week at different times of the day. Now, I have more familiarity with the process, and it takes me less time to discover the pattern. Many of the patterns I observe are ones I have seen before; however, I have also seen many diverse patterns over the years. One of the reasons I like to have someone else observe the same student is because it's sometimes easy to not see your own responses to the inappropriate behavior. Teachers have said to me, "I had no idea I was doing that!"

The Student's Behavior Serves a Purpose

When students repeatedly engage in inappropriate behavior, it is because the behavior is serving a purpose for the students. The students

Figure 6.2 ABC Observation

Student _____ Student ID _____

Date _____ Setting _____

Reason for Observation _____

Time	A—Antecedent	B—Behavior	C—Consequence	Observer Initials

Observer's Name _____

are getting something that they want (Umbreit et al., 2007). What students want can often be surprising.

One day several years ago I was traveling and had just completed a seminar on child abuse. I got in the car and was driving back to Houston when I got hungry. I pulled over to a large restaurant on the side of the road. I went inside and sat at a booth. A young couple and their son came into the restaurant and sat down in the booth in front of me. They really stood out because they were very unkempt. Both the mom and dad had on T-shirts that looked like they had once been white and clean. Now they were grey and stained and looked like they had not been washed in a long time. Their jeans looked the same. Their son looked like he was about two years old. He had on nothing but a diaper and the diaper very obviously needed changing. His little body and his hair were filthy. He sat to the side of his parents. They kept talking, but ignored him. He started whining, and they still ignored him. He grabbed his daddy's T-shirt while whining some more, but he still was ignored. His whining got louder and louder and he still was ignored. They just kept talking to each other like he was not even there. He started pulling harder on his dad's dirty T-shirt, whining louder, and suddenly his dad turned around to face him, raised his hand, and gave his son a big smack. For one brief moment, the little boy gave a huge smile as if to say, "My dad noticed me," and then he started crying harder, probably from the pain of the slap. I watched all of this in silent horror, wishing I could do something for that little boy. The point of the story is that this is a clear case of the behavior serving a very unusual purpose. The antecedent in this case was the parents ignoring the child. The behavior was the child whining and pulling on his dad's T-shirt. The consequence was that he was noticed. It was a negative way, but for him it was a payoff: he was noticed. The consequences of inappropriate behavior are not always positive.

Here are some of the consequences you may see when you observe students. You may see students engaging in inappropriate behavior to get the attention of their peers. I have seen children who argue with their teacher to get other students to laugh at the teacher. I have seen students who bully, and they get the attention of not only of their victims, but also of their peers.

Some students may pick fights so that others will leave them alone. They do not want to interact with others. They get their wish as students do ignore them.

Some students engage in inappropriate behavior to get a concrete reward. Jason was one of those students. He had tantrums so both his parents and his teacher would give in to him and give him anything he asked for. He got a new bicycle this way from his parents.

Still other students are argumentative with their teachers or peers so that they get out of something. Patrick did not want to do his homework. He argued with his teacher, and she finally gave in and said, "OK, no homework tonight." He did the same thing with his parents when he did not want to do something. His mom wanted him to do chores at home. He argued with her, and then he didn't have to do the chores.

Some children are sensitive to sensory stimuli—things in their environment. Jenna cries so that her mom will hug her and rub her back. It works. Candice cries whenever the radio or television is on in her home. She can't stand the noise. Her mom immediately turns off the television. At school, she cries when it is noisy so she can be sent to the calming station because it is quieter there.

You can see from these examples that in all the cases, students engaged in the inappropriate behavior to either gain something or to avoid something (Umbreit et al., 2007). The important thing is that it works for the students. The more it works, the more they will do it again.

Observe the behavior, and you will have your answer as to which of the consequences the student is receiving as a function of the inappropriate behavior (see Figure 6.3).

Once you know the antecedent and the consequence, it is time to design an intervention. The intervention will need to either be a new replacement behavior, a change in the environment, or a different consequence when the student engages in the inappropriate behavior.

In all cases the intervention will have to address either the antecedent or the consequence in order for there to be a new behavior. The intervention needs to be based on assessment of the individual student's needs. This means it has to be customized because every student is unique, and as I said earlier, what works for one student may not work for another.

The intervention has to be able to be implemented within the inclusive general education classroom, especially for the first two tiers of RTI. Sometimes, in the third tier, it may be necessary to have a student go out of the classroom for awhile each day to work on the problem behavior.

There are considerations in designing the Intervention Plan. It has to be focused on long-term results. The goal is for the student to not just engage in appropriate behavior in the general education classroom during this school year, but to have the skills to engage in appropriate behavior throughout the years of school and even for a lifetime.

Figure 6.3 Gains or Avoids Worksheet

Does the Student Gain or Avoid Something?

	Gain	Avoid
Attention		
Concrete Reward or Activity		
Sensory Stimulation		

The intervention has to be respectful (Bambara & Kern, 2005). It has to be carefully thought out by the RTI team so there is never any feeling of embarrassment for the student.

Progress Monitoring (PBIS)

Number of Occurrences

Assessment is the cornerstone of PBIS. One way to do this is to chart the number of occurrences of an inappropriate behavior prior to the intervention, and then chart it every couple of days once the intervention has been implemented. Every time the student engages in the inappropriate behavior, a check is put into a box. Total the number of checks at the end of the day. The goal is to have fewer and fewer checks (see Figure 6.4).

Duration of Occurrences

Sometimes it is useful to track the length of time a student engages in the inappropriate behavior. You may find when you are tracking the frequency of the behavior, that the frequency may not diminish as much, but the duration of the inappropriate behavior becomes shorter and shorter. For example, the inappropriate behavior may have initially lasted for five minutes, but with the intervention, it now occurs for only two minutes. See Figure 6.5 to track the length of time the behavior lasts.

Permanent Products

Permanent product data is data that is available at schools (Riley-Tillman, Kalberer, & Chafouleas, 2005). For example, track the number of discipline referrals following an intervention. If school attendance was an issue prior to the intervention, track the number of days the student is absent following implementing the intervention. Still another example of permanent data is homework completion. For example, prior to the intervention, this was a real problem with William. He turned in his homework only 10 percent of the time. Now the records indicate that William turns in completed homework 75 percent of the time.

Professional Behavioral Programs

In addition to the methods shown here for screening and progress monitoring, there are professionally purchased programs available for progress monitoring and universal screening of behavior. Consult the back of this book for organizations and resources.

Figure 6.4 Frequency Assessment

Name of Student _____ Student ID _____

Observer(s) _____ Date _____

The behavior being monitored is _____

_____

Observer Initials	1	2	3	4	5	6	7	8	9	10	Time of Assessment

Total occurrences _____

Figure 6. 5 Extent of Time Assessment

Name of Student _____ Student ID _____

Observer(s) _____ Date _____

The behavior being monitored is _____

_____

Starting Time	Ending Time	Observer Initials

Total occurrences _____

Antecedent
Interventions

7

Children are like roses that thrive when loved and tended.

—Maryln Appelbaum

Antecedents are the events that appear right before problem behaviors occur. Change the antecedent and frequently the behavior changes (Umbreit et al., 2007). The antecedents you will be learning about in this chapter are supported by research evidence. Many of these interventions will help students academically. Once they stop misbehaving, they can learn better. They go hand-in-hand. These are all Tier 1 interventions to be implemented in the general education classroom by the general education teacher.

ATTENTION ANTECEDENTS

When I ask teachers what the number one reason that students misbehave is, I frequently hear, "They want attention." They may want the attention from the teacher, or they may want it from their peers. The way they get it, however, is to act out. There are several effective interventions for this.

Scheduled Attention of Teacher

I can still vividly remember the first time I ever heard about this intervention. I was doing an all-day seminar on ADHD. It was early in the morning before the seminar started. I always make it a point to walk around the room and greet all of the participants, shaking hands and making conversation. I started that day at the back of the room and moved to the front, and in the front row, there was a woman who warmly greeted me and said, "I have ADHD." We talked for a few minutes and then she told me that because the administration at her school knew she had ADHD, they felt she was best suited to handle students with ADHD. They therefore gave her a class that included eight students, all boys, with ADHD. I asked her how she was doing with her class. She told me that she was doing great. She said she knew that she would have to hold their attention, or they would misbehave. She said the first week of school she gave each of the boys some type of attention, like eye contact, a little sticky note with a smiley face, or words of encouragement, every three minutes. She said that she gradually extended that time to four minutes, then five minutes, and now, she said that her students were doing fine with very little attention from her. This is a great example of using scheduled attention (Kern, 1995).

Scheduled Attention of Peers

There are students who seem to crave attention from other students. There are several ways to handle this. First, discover which student's attention is wanted. Collin was one of those students who seemed to crave the attention of his peers. At first, I thought he wanted the attention of the entire class, but then I noticed that it was just one other student, Rob. I observed that when Rob was absent, Collin did not misbehave. Yet, when Rob was there, Collin would become disruptive and then check Rob's facial expression see his reaction. Rob always had a major reaction, laughing loudly. I had them become peer mentors. This meant that every fifteen minutes, they would each take turns highlighting what had been learned. Collin's disruptive behavior disappeared. He did not need to do it anymore because he was already getting Rob's attention.

Another way you can handle this is to have students do cooperative learning activities, or arrange similar students in flexible groups to work on projects together.

Proximity Control

Proximity control is extremely effective for attention-getting behavior (Gunter & Shores, 1995). There are two ways to implement this. The first way is to seat students who have a tendency to be disruptive in closer proximity to you. It has been my experience that they generally prefer to hide out at the back of the room. When they are near the teacher their attention-getting behavior decreases.

The second way is to leave them where they are seated, but you move closer to them while teaching. This has been extremely effective. You do not have to say anything to them specifically, just walk over and stand near them as you talk to the rest of the class.

Highly Preferred Activities

Highly preferred activities are activities that are interesting to students and hold their attention (Cipani, 1993). There are times in the classroom when the work may seem dull or monotonous. Natalie got into trouble because she would constantly get out of her seat, walk over to the pencil sharpener where her teacher, Mr. Klein, kept a stack of pencils, and stand there noisily sharpening them over and over again. Mr. Klein tracked the number of occurrences and found that Natalie engaged in this behavior for nearly one-fourth of the class period daily. He discussed this behavior with the intervention team, and they designed a Tier 1 intervention to be implemented within his classroom. Mr. Klein gave Natalie a timer, told her to do her work, and set the timer for every fifteen minutes. When the timer went off, she was allowed to stand up and sharpen one pencil in the pencil stack. She then returned to her seat. Just that one brief highly preferred activity was enough to keep Natalie engaged during seat times. Mr. Klein gradually lengthened the time on task to thirty minutes.

I believe students would prefer that both you and their peers think they are bad, rather than think they are "dumb." When they cannot do something, they often misbehave to divert attention from the situation that is causing them to feel like a failure. Look for ways to make their task more interesting using activities they prefer, and their behavior often changes.

Student Choice

Remember earlier I said there were students who engaged in disruptive behavior to avoid tasks. An effective way to engage these students is to offer them a "voice." This is an effective way to reduce inappropriate behaviors (Kern et al., 1998).

I use student choice when dealing with strong-willed students who want constant attention. I do not get caught up in their arguments. Instead, I say, "You can do . . . or . . . . Which do you choose to do?" I offer them two positive choices. For example, I might say, "You can do your math assignment now, or you can do the reading assignment now, and the math later. Which one do you choose?"

Task Difficulty

When work is too hard, students have a difficult time sitting still and act out to get away from their work (Gunter & Denny, 1996). Decrease the difficulty of the work, and often the problem behavior stops.

Meaningful Learning

When you watch television, you choose programs that have meaning to you. When you go to the movies, you choose movies that are meaningful and interesting to you. Students do not get this choice. They are told what they will be learning, and then they are taught it. Teachers also have no choice in the curriculum; however, there is choice in how it is presented, and it can be presented in a meaningful way. The more meaningful it is to students, the more likely they will be to listen and learn, and not engage in disruptive behavior (Dunlap, Kern-Dunlap, Clark, & Robbins, 1991).

Changing the Style

The goal is to have students complete an assignment. For some students, this can be a struggle and they then misbehave. It may not be the assignment that is causing the problem. It is instead the way they are required to do it (Kern, Childs, Dunlap, Clarke, & Falk, 1994). For example, there are some students who have a very difficult time with handwriting assignments. They erase them over and over again. When given a computer on which to do assignments, they get the job done without misbehaving.

Consistency

Consistency is very important for students. They need the predictability of knowing what will happen and when it will happen (Clark, Worcester, Dunlap, Murray, & Bradley-Klug, 2002). When events occur that are unscheduled, it can throw off their entire day. This is especially true with students who engage in inappropriate behavior. Most teachers will tell you that when there is a substitute, students have a tendency to engage in more inappropriate behaviors. That is because it is a change. When there is a fire drill, they also have a tendency to engage in more inappropriate behaviors. Once again, it is a change in the routine.

Imagine that you get on an airplane to fly to Hawaii. You are very excited about the trip. It is scheduled to last seven hours. The plane takes off, and in a few minutes the pilot says, "Ladies and gentlemen, we have decided to break the trip into three segments. We will be landing in three different cities and staying overnight in each of them. We will arrive in

Hawaii in three nights. Have a pleasant trip." Would you be annoyed? Do you think you might engage in some behavior that the pilot would consider inappropriate? That is exactly what happens with students when their predictable schedule is altered. Say what you mean to students, and mean what you say. Students need to know what will be happening during their day.

Change the Instructional Delivery

Your tone of voice is very important (Wasley, Hampel, & Clark, 1997). Students may engage in inappropriate behavior because of the way they hear things. I knew a teacher who was a delightful woman. She truly cared about the children. However, she had problems with classroom management. When she spoke, it was in a flat voice. She did not vary her voice tone. Students got bored and misbehaved. I have heard other teachers who speak to students in a manner that is not inviting. Students become resentful when they are constantly ordered to do things. They need to be told in firm yet respectful tones what they need to do.

Warn Students Ahead

When you know there is going to be a transition or a change in routine, warn students ahead of time. Use multiple warnings (Mace, Shapiro, & Mace, 1998). "In ten minutes, it will be time to put your work away." Then later say, "In five minutes, it will be time to put your work away." Still later say, "In one minute, it will be time to put your work away."

Transition Activities

It can be difficult for students to stop doing something they enjoy doing. They are focused and then if they suddenly have to change what they are doing, they may misbehave. Schedule a transitional activity to reduce the problem (McIntosh, Herman, Sanford, McGraw, & Florence, 2004). The transition activity needs to be an activity that students enjoy doing.

Accessibility of Items

Students may misbehave when they become frustrated because they cannot reach something they want, or the object is not available (Bambara & Kern, 2005). Ensure that items are not too high up where they cannot reach them. If there are items that students fight over, you may want to have duplicates of those items so that more students can use them at the same time.

Alternative Methods of Stimulation

Angela was a student who her hands in her mouth all the time. It seriously impacted her social life because students were afraid of being touched by her. She needed an alternative method for the stimulation she was receiving from her fingers in her mouth. A box of straws was placed on her desk within easy reach. When she felt like sucking her fingers, she instead reached for a straw. When she was finished, she tossed the straw out.

Other students who move around a lot benefit from exercise. Including movement in your class instruction can prevent behavior problems from occurring (Kern, Koegel, Dyer, Blew, & Fenton, 1982).

TEACHER-STUDENT RELATIONSHIP

Student-teacher relationships make a difference in student behavior (Marzano et al., 2003). Many behavioral problems begin because of a breakdown in relationships between the teacher and students (Sheets & Gay, 1996). While characteristics like consideration, patience, and enthusiasm are important, the two most important aspects of effective teacher-student relationships are dominance and cooperation (Wubbles, Brekelmans, Van Tartwijk, & Admiral, 1999).

Teacher Dominance and Control

Teachers who are dominant in the classroom have a strong sense of purpose and strong guidance of students (Marzano, 2003). They take charge. When this is combined with the second characteristic of cooperation—caring about the needs of students and what they think, and wanting to work together with them as a team—it is powerful.

Concern for the Individual Needs of Student

There is yet another very important characteristic of teachers who are more effective at classroom management. They take into consideration that every student is different and use different strategies for different students (Brophy, 1996). Every student is truly different. It is estimated that as many as 60 to 70 percent of students who are referred for behavior problems have a history of physical or sexual abuse (Thompson & Wyatt, 1999). Still other students suffer from depression or other emotional issues. They are not "one size fits all" kids. They need and deserve to be treated in a way that helps them to succeed. Teachers can achieve control, dominance, and cooperation, and still meet the individual needs of their students.

Be Assertive

Being assertive is a key element in taking control. Assertiveness is the ability to stand up for what you believe without infringing on the rights of others (Emmer et al., as cited by Marzano, 2003). There are various components of assertive behavior. Body language is an important component. I tell teachers to stand and walk "tall" regardless of their height. Imagine that you have two people in front of you. They are both dressed identically. They are both saying the same thing. One of them is standing up straight, and the other one is slumped over. Which one would you listen to the most? You would listen to the one who is standing straight and confidently.

The words and tone are other important components in assertiveness (Appelbaum, 2002). When you want a student to listen to you, use a firm yet caring deep voice. I believe students respond better to a deep voice than to a high, shrill voice. Use assertive statements to ask for what you need (Appelbaum, 2002). First, state the student's name, and then say what you need or what you would appreciate. Have your voice get deeper and lower as you speak.

"Omer, I would appreciate . . ."

"Brinna, I need you to . . ."

Connect

Take time to connect with each student (Hargreaves, 2000). I realize that some of you reading this book may have many students, and you may think this would be difficult. I have an analogy for you. Imagine going to a large, local supermarket every week to shop for your groceries. You see the same stockers, packers, manager, and cash register associates week after week. Everyone is busy doing his or her own individual job. You have shopped there for years, but you do not know the names of anyone who works there, and they don't know your name. Now imagine that a brand new supermarket opens up nearby. You go into the store, and you find the prices and the products are the same. There is a major difference, though. When you walk in the door of the new store, the employees smile at you. They make you feel welcome. As you are walking down the aisle, a clerk comes up to you, and says, "How can I help you?" When you get in line to check out, the person who works at the cash register smiles at you and says, "How are you doing today? Did you find everything all right? My name is Maria, and I hope to see you here again." Which store would become your favorite? I can tell you that my favorite would be the one where I was made to feel welcome, and where people took a personal interest in me. It is the same with students (McCombs & Whisler, as cited by Marzano, 2003).

I have an intervention that I use for the toughest student in my classes. I set aside a special time every day to meet with that student for three weeks. The meeting only lasts for three to five minutes, but it is a powerful connecting experience. I tell the student initially, "I want to get to know you better, so we will be meeting daily for the next three weeks." I find a time that works for both of us to meet alone. This is a special time—a time to get to know the student. I don't talk about rules or class work. Instead the student talks and tells me information. I ask questions such as, "What do you like to do?" and "What is your favorite television program?" All of my questions are designed to get to know the student better. I believe that the more you connect, the less you correct. This is a really good antecedent intervention. It totally changes the relationship with the student. When the relationship changes, then the student's behavior changes.

Alternative Skill Interventions 8

Success breeds success.

—Maryln Appelbaum

During a consultation I went into a fourth-grade classroom to work with the students. I had all the students gathered around me in a large circle. My goal was to demonstrate to the teachers how to talk to students so they would listen. As part of the conversation, students started telling me their problems with inappropriate behaviors. They knew which behaviors got them into trouble, and they asked if I could help them stay out of trouble. They were all eager to have solutions. The solutions that I gave them were all alternatives to the problem behaviors. One boy, Aaron, said that he tapped his pen or pencil repeatedly. He said he couldn't stop. He just had to tap. I suggested that when he felt like tapping, he tap on a sponge so that the noise would not distract anyone. I have used this same method of providing alternative skill interventions for elementary and secondary students. This chapter is packed with alternative skill interventions.

My above example was a "quick fix" to help students. They were very receptive, but the ideal way to do this is to use the RTI format of assessing students, observing them, and forming a hypothesis statement about why the behavior is occurring. Once you have the hypothesis statement, an intervention can be designed. This chapter assumes that you have carried out the observation and assessment, and now only need to plug in the interventions.

REPLACEMENT BEHAVIOR

Teaching a replacement behavior for the former problem behavior is an alternative skill intervention (Horner & Day, 1991). The new replacement behavior becomes a substitute for the former behavior. This assumes that the antecedent conditions are the same. For example, Aaron, the boy who taps his pencil, may tap it whenever he has to concentrate on a task. The antecedent is the task that requires concentration. The behavior is the pencil tapping. The antecedent remains the same, but Aaron is engaging in a new behavior, tapping the pencil on a sponge, and the consequence is totally different. Before, Aaron got in trouble every time he tapped his pencil on the desk because of the noise it made. Now, he is not making any noise, and he does not get into any trouble (see Figure 8.1).

Depending on the replacement behavior, this can be a Tier 1 or Tier 2 intervention. If it is a complex replacement behavior, it is Tier 2. If it is something that can be easily implemented by the general education teacher, it is a Tier 1 intervention.

Figure 8.1 Aaron's Old Behavior and Aaron's New Behavior

Antecedent	Behavior	Consequence
Concentrating on task	*Old Behavior* Pencil tapping on desk	Get in trouble
Concentrating on task	*New Behavior* Pencil tapping on sponge	Stay positive and keep working on task

Rehearse and Prompt Behavior

The ideal way to teach a replacement behavior is to have the student rehearse it. Teach the student what to do, and then have the student practice doing it during a time when the antecedent condition is not present. Then remind the student about the new behavior, and re-introduce the antecedent condition. In the example I gave you earlier, the antecedent condition is concentration on a task. Therefore, the new behavior is taught during a time when Aaron does not have to concentrate. Later, when he has practiced the new behavior, the antecedent condition is re-introduced. Aaron's teacher reminds him that when he is concentrating and wants to tap his pencil, to tap it on the sponge. If Aaron forgets, his teacher can gently but firmly remind him. This is called prompting the new behavior (Morgan, Whorton, & Willets, 2000). Depending on the amount of prompting that needs to be taught, this could be a Tier 1 or Tier 2 intervention.

Replacement Behavior With Little or No Effort

It's important when you use a replacement behavior as an intervention that it does not require a lot of extra effort on the student's part, or the student will not want to do it (Horner & Day, 1991). The example I gave with the pencil tapping took the same amount of effort as when Aaron tapped his pencil on the desk. Look for a replacement behavior that is the same or even less effort than the problem behavior so it is simple for the student to do.

Students Who Need Movement

There are great benefits to be found from exercise (Cai, 2000). It creates a state of well being that counters anxiety and depression, and can have a positive affect on student behavior. These are all Tier 1 forms of physical activity that can be done within the general education classroom.

Stretch Break

Every thirty minutes have a stretch break for all students to stand up and stretch for a minute. That little stretch can make a big difference.

Stress Ball

Have a stress ball that students can squeeze when they have the urge to move around. I have seen students squeeze the ball over and over again, and they are able to concentrate and behave better. I believe some students take all their frustrations out on the ball.

Velcro

Attach a piece of Velcro to the bottom of a student's desk. Have the student rub on the Velcro to release tension. It's another small way of providing some movement—some exercise.

Rocking Chair

Have a cozy corner in the room with a rocking chair. Have a timer beside the chair. Students set the timer when they sit down and rock back and forth until the timer has gone off. My favorite timers are liquid ones because they do not make noise.

Empty Desk

Have an empty desk near the front of the classroom. Students who need some movement can get up, move to the empty desk, and work there for a while as long as they do not disturb any other students going between desks. When they need to move again, they go back to their own desks.

Asking Permission for Movement

There are students who cannot work for long periods of time on the same thing. They just have to move. Their trigger is the extended time on a task. These students then act out by disrupting the class. Their disruption serves the purpose of getting them out of having to do the task for a while. A replacement behavior for these students is to teach them how to ask appropriately for help (Reichle, Drager, & Davis, 2002). They can be taught to say, "I need help." They will need to practice so that it becomes a new way of helping themselves. Candice often was very frustrated when she had to do seatwork in math. When she became frustrated, she got out of her seat, walked over to other students, and pushed or even hit them. Her teacher, Ms. Collins, observed her, and found that she sat well when she was learning other subjects. The problem was seatwork in math. She taught Candice to use her words, "I need help," when she became frustrated, and the problem behavior ended.

Signal to Ask for Movement

Teach students a signal to ask for some time off from concentration—some movement—rather than engaging in inappropriate disruptive behavior. Traffic light signals are visible for teachers to see. Use bright red squares that are six inches by six inches on laminated poster board. Students keep them in their desk until they are needed. When they need to take a breather, they put them on their desk as a signal to ask for that relaxing time.

It is important when students take their breather that they do not get into further trouble. Teach them appropriate behavior. They can sit and breathe deeply, go to the bathroom, or take one lap around the room. Whatever it is, it should fit the needs of the student. For some students, it would be better to just sit in their seats and breathe deeply. If they got up, they might have a tendency to not return to their desks. The intervention team needs to decide this. The replacement behavior needs to be rehearsed with the student so that he or she becomes accustomed to it. This may be either a Tier 1 or Tier 2 intervention.

SELF-MANAGEMENT SKILLS

Students need to learn how to handle their emotions. They need to learn how to handle stress, anger, and social problems. They also need to learn how to set goals for themselves and work to reach those goals. Self-management skills are a fundamental key to success not only in the class-room, but also in life.

Stress Management—Relaxation Training

Deep Breathing

Teach students to breathe deeply. It reduces stress. Have students prac-tice. They take a deep breath into their abdomens. They hold it for a few seconds, and then they slowly release their breath. I have them practice it over and over again. This is an effective strategy before a test or any other stressful time. This can be a Tier 1 intervention taught to the entire class.

Music

Music has the ability to calm students (Hallam & Price, 1998). Have you ever gotten into your car at the end of the day feeling stressed? You turn on the radio or CD player, listen to some music, and your mood instantly changes. That is what it can do for students too. There have been many studies on the effects of music. One study showed that students with emotional and behavioral problems had a decrease in problem behaviors when they heard music (Hallam & Price, 1998). The students listened to Mozart during times when they did math problems. Prior to the music, they would get out of their seats without permission, hit other students, address their teacher without permission, and make excessive noise like banging objects. When the music was playing, their entire bodies changed. There were changes in body temperature, breathing rate, blood pressure, and pulse—all while listening to Mozart. They performed better on their math problems while the music was playing in the background. They also obeyed the rules better and were more cooperative and less aggressive. This study makes a strong case for using music in your classroom. When I observe classrooms, I, too, see a calming affect on the students from music.

There are several ways you can use music. You can have it playing in the background to calm the entire class, or you can have the student who needs to relax listen to music via headphones. You can have a relaxation station in your classroom that has headphones with music. All of these are Tier 1 interventions.

Just as you have a favorite tune that relaxes you, so too do students. Have them tell you which song calms them. That is the song they can sing to themselves without any sound when they feel stressed. They say the words over and over again in their heads until they feel calm. This is a strategy that may take practice and can either be a Tier 1 or Tier 2 intervention.

Options Training

Teach students to recognize the events that are "trigger" events—events that cause them to engage in inappropriate behavior. They do not generally realize they have options, or that there are other ways they can respond to the trigger situation. Teach them to define the choices (Kern et al., 1998). Have them state the problem to themselves: "I cannot do my homework." Then have them state to themselves all the things they can do:

- "I can have a tantrum to get out of it."
- "I can ask my parents to help me."
- "I can tell my teacher tomorrow that I need help understanding the subject."
- "I can take some deep breaths, relax, and start over."

Once they have identified all their options, they can make a decision about what will be the best option for them. This is a skill that will help them not only in the classroom, but also in every situation in their lives. They are learning how to think for themselves. This can be a Tier 1 intervention taught to the entire class, or it may be part of an Intervention Plan for Tier 2.

Self-Talk for Anger Management

There are some students who become easily frustrated. The first step in anger management is to teach students how to recognize when they are angry (Bambara & Kern, 2005). I have had students who became angry and raged, but when I spoke to them about it, they would say, "I wasn't angry." I realized that I had to teach them to recognize the characteristics of being angry so they would know when it happened. I taught them to check their bodies and their thoughts. Their faces may become red and hot to the touch. Their thinking may become clouded. Their pulses may race. They often have to move; to do something with the rage inside. They cannot stop what they cannot recognize. The other thing I have noticed is some students will say, "I wasn't angry, I was just frustrated." I never argue with them. It is their word for the angry feelings they have, and I can still work with that. I then shift to talking about recognizing when they are frustrated. I teach them to recognize their "triggers," the antecedent conditions that cause them to become frustrated or angry.

Now they are ready to learn self-talk. Self-talk is the words you say to yourself. Students who use negative self-talk are more likely to have increased anxiety. Increased anxiety affects functioning and is more likely to increase negative behaviors (Kendall & Treadwell, 2007). Positive self-talk can be an effective tool for achieving self-control. When students change the words they say to themselves, they will change their feeling and their moods. I create a self-talk list for students to use. It has statements that are calming, such as the following:

- "I am becoming calmer."
- "I can handle this."
- "I breathe deeply and relax."
- "My words and actions are relaxed and appropriate."
- "I feel better and better."
- "I am relaxed."

They choose the self-talk words off a sheet filled with statements, or they may reach into an "Anger Management Bag." The bag is filled with slips of paper. They pull out a slip and read it over and over again until they feel calm. This is generally a Tier 2 intervention.

Peer Mediation

I have been mostly talking about students whose behaviors are disruptive. There is another group of students who are socially withdrawn. These may be students who have lost their confidence because of schoolwork or because of difficult home life situations. They need help too. Their social lives are important to them. Peers play an important part in the lives of students and an important role in helping students who are socially isolated (Christensen, Young, & Marchant, 2004).

Positive Peer Reporting (PPR)

This is an effective strategy for helping isolated students learn new social skills (Christensen, Young, & Marchant, 2007). Start with choosing a peer partner for the socially isolated student. This needs to be someone who will help the student be successful. Zach was extremely withdrawn. He spoke little in the classroom. He had no friends. He was a quiet, shy child. The RTI intervention team decided to implement PPR for Zach as one of his interventions. They chose Carl to be his peer partner. Carl had good social skills; seemed like a positive, upbeat student; avoided negative interactions; got along well with his teachers; and followed directions well. He was one of those students who never missed school. He also seemed to like Zach, and demonstrated this with kind acts toward Zach on several different occasions.

Carl and Zach were told they were to work together as a team to help Zach learn social skills. The teacher gave them both a list of several skills that Zach was learning. The list was objectively written as a check sheet. It included items such as the following:

- Looks at the teacher when the teacher is speaking
- Answers questions orally when asked
- Reads aloud so that people within two feet can hear him

When Zach began an academic assignment, Carl started watching while also doing his own assignment. At five-minute intervals, he recorded the items that had occurred with a check. He was given a little timer so he knew when it had been five minutes. Every time Carl checked off one of the positive interactions, he made a positive comment to Zach about the appropriate behavior, such as, "Great job, Zach!" or "Way to go!" When Zach finished his work, he brought it to Carl to review. If Zach had finished his work and done it accurately, Carl would say a positive remark like, "Good job." He might even hand Carl some token points every time he did a good job.

Check-In and Check-Out (CICO)

This is a program that has been found to be effective for students who have tougher behavior problems and do not respond to general classroom strategies (Hawken & Horner, 2003). It is generally a Tier 2 or Tier 3 intervention. Students who are in the CICO program check in every morning with a designated teacher. They develop a behavioral goal for the day and have a point card they carry with them. At designated times throughout the day, the students check in and are given points on their point card if their behavior is on target. This ensures students get feedback all day about their behavior. At the end of the day, students check out and see if their behavioral goal was met. It is designed to be a positive experience. Even if the goal was not met, students hear positive words of encouragement from the teacher. When students check out, they receive a behavioral note to take home for their parents that shows how many points they received throughout the day. Their parents sign it, students return it the next day, and the process begins again.

The points students earn are collected and traded at least once a week at designated times. They are traded for prizes, activities, or free time.

This is effective because of the many ways students are reinforced throughout the process. They receive prompts to engage in appropriate behavior when they set their daily goals. They get increased feedback all day as they are given points. It provides structure for student behavior on the cards, sets expectations, and it involves the parents.

EXAMPLE OF THREE TIERS IN BEHAVIOR MANAGEMENT

Kyle had a problem with anger management. He had tantrums in the classroom. He raised his voice, kicked chairs, hit his desk or walls, and threw things when angry. Initially there was a brief assessment in which Kyle was screened using the ABC Observation Sheet, the Frequency Assessment, and the Student Gains or Avoids Assessment. It was determined that the antecedent was when Kyle saw something he wanted, he would engage in tantrum behavior. The consequence was that he almost always got what he wanted. It had become a learned pattern.

Mrs. Jeffers referred Kyle to the RTI team and together they designed an Intervention Plan for Kyle for Tier 1. The plan was designed to be preventative. It included Mrs. Jeffers establishing a connection with Kyle so he would feel more comfortable asking for what he wanted rather than having tantrums. Rehearsing and prompting more appropriate behavior, options training, and self-talk were also included in Tier 1. Frequent progress monitoring determined that it was not effective. They did an additional, more in-depth screening and designed a Tier 2 intervention plan that was implemented by an interventionist for Kyle. They still reinforced the interventions for Tier 1, but now included check-in, check-out for Tier 2. While progress monitoring showed that Kyle's behavior improved, it still did not improve sufficiently. Kyle's mother attended the RTI team meeting to discuss implementing Tier 3. The team discovered that Kyle's father was in the army and just recently had been declared missing in action. The team decided to add Tier 3, an individualized intensive intervention of meeting with the school counselor twice a week to talk about what was happening. This, in addition to the other interventions, proved to be extremely effective. Kyle's behavior improved. Interestingly, when his behavior improved, his academic work improved too.

Figure 8.2 Three Tiers of Behavior Management for Kyle

Tier	Intervention(s)	Location	Time	Person	Duration
1	• Connection • Options Training • Self-Talk • Rehearse and Prompt	General education classroom	30 minutes	General education teacher	4 times a week for 10 weeks
2	• Check-In, Check-Out	Outside of classroom	30 minutes	Interventionist	Daily for 10 weeks
3	• Counseling	Outside of classroom	60 minutes	School counselor as interventionist	2 times a week for 10 weeks

Conclusion

I started this book by saying that RTI will revolutionize education. It will. It is a recipe for success with students. Like most recipes, it takes time and effort to create. It has all of the ingredients for success. These ingredients that need to be pulled together are universal screening, tiered instruction, progress monitoring, collaboration, and research-based academic and behavioral interventions, all within a differentiated classroom. It also needs a liberal sprinkling of professional development, fidelity of implementation, and parental involvement.

The recipe will take patience, professional development, knowledge, skills, motivation, and dedication to create. But the end result is a world of difference for students who formerly struggled. This recipe creates achievement, hope, and motivation for success. It is the most worthwhile recipe ever created for the students of America.

Resources

General Information About RTI

Council of Administrators of Special Education
http://www.casecec.org/rti.htm

National Association for State Directors of Special Education
http://www.nasdse.org

National Association of School Psychologists
http://www.nasponline.org

National Center for Learning Disabilities
http://www.ncld.org/org/content/view/1002/389/

Academic Interventions and Resources

AIMSweb
http://www.Aimsweb.com
They offer assessment materials for curriculum-based measurement.

Big Ideas in Beginning Reading
http://reading.uoregon.edu/curricula/or_rfc_reveiw.php
This is a Web site all about literacy.

Council for Exceptional Children
http://www.cec.sped.org
This organization is dedicated to improving educational outcomes for all individuals with disabilities and exceptionalities.

Curriculum-Based Measurement Support for K–12
http://www.cbmnow.com/
Their Web site is all about curriculum-based measurement.

Dynamic Indicators of Basic Early Literacy Skills (DIBELS)
http://www.dibels.uoregon.edu
They have standardized and individualized short reading assessments.

Florida Center for Reading Research
http://www.fcrr.org
They have information on assessments and evaluate reading programs.

Institute for the Development of Educational Achievement, University
of Oregon
http://reading.uoregon.edu/appendices/con_guide_3.1.03.pdf
They have a guide to evaluating reading programs.

Institute of Education Science, What Works Clearinghouse
http://ies.ed.gov/ncee/wwc/
This is a federal agency that funds research on effective practices. You
will find many research-based programs listed on their Web site and
ratings for those programs.

International Reading Association
http://www.reading.org/
They provide information to support research, and are a support for
all those who teach reading.

IRIS Center for Training Enhancements
http://iris.peabody.vanderbilt.edu/index.html
They have free online interactive training, and RTI is one of their topics.

Journal of Evidence-Based Practices for Schools
http://www.rowmaneducation.com/Journals/JEBP/Index.shtml
They offer research-based articles for educators.

National Center for Student Progress Monitoring
http://www.studentprogress.org/
They are a source on scientifically based student monitoring in an RTI
framework.

National Center on Response to Intervention
http://www.rti4success.org/
Their goal is to provide assistance in implementing RTI.

Office of Special Education Programs, Ideas That Work
http://www.osepideasthatwork.org/
They are sponsored by the federal government and have a toolkit that
offers many ideas for both academic and behavioral RTI.

RTI Action Network
http://rtinetwork.org/
They are affiliated with many national organizations and are a program of the National Center for Learning Disabilities, offering information and networking for implementing RTI.

Regional Resource and Federal Center Network
http://www.rrfcnetwork.org/component/option,com_bookmarks/Itemid,28model,0/catid,83navstart,0/search,*
They assist state educational agencies with improving education for children with disabilities.

Sopris West
http://www.sopriswest.com/
This is a source for intervention and assessment.

Vaughn Gross Center for Reading and Language Arts
http://www.texasreading.org/utcrla/
They research reading and language programs.

Behavioral Interventions and Resources

Association for Positive Behavior Supports
http://www.apbs.org
This is an international association that promotes research-based behavioral interventions.

Center for Developmental Disabilities at the University of Kansas
http://uappbs.apbs.org
They offer online positive behavior support modules.

Center for Evidence-Based Practice: Young Children with Challenging Behavior
http://www.challengingbehavior.org.fmhi.usf.edu
They promote evidence-based research for young children with behavior problems.

Council for Children With Behavior Disorders
http://www.ccbd.net
Their journal, Beyond Behavior, is practitioner-based and integrated with RTI and PBIS.

Journal of Positive Behavior Interventions
http://www.ingentaconnect.com/content/proedcw/jpbi
They publish research with practical examples of schools that have implemented specific academic and behavioral strategies.

Office of Special Education Programs, Ideas that Work
http://www.osepideasthatwork.org/
They are sponsored by the federal government and have a toolkit that offers many ideas for both academic and behavioral RTI.

PBIS – Understanding Problem Behavior
http://serc.gws.uky.edu/pbis
This is an interactive tutorial on problem behavior and supports.

Positive Behavioral Interventions and Supports
http://www.pbis.org/main.htm
This is an excellent resource on the positive behavior interventions and supports for RTI.

Schoolwide Information System
http://www.swis.org
This is a Web-based system for schools to use office referral data to design both individual and school-wide interventions.

Squidoo's Positive School Climate Web site
http://www.squidoo.com/PBIS
This has schoolwide PBIS, classroom systems, individual student support systems, and more.

Some Statewide Positive Behavior Support Web Sites

Colorado Positive Behavior Support
http://www.cde.state.co.us/pbs/

Delaware's Positive Behavior Support Project
http://www.udel.edu/cds/pbs/

Florida's PBS Project
http://flpbs.fmhi.usf.edu/

Illinois Statewide Technical Assistance Center
http://www.pbisillinois.org

Kentucky's Behavior Home Page
http://www.state.ky.us/agencies/behave/homepage.html

Maryland's Positive Behavioral Interventions and Supports
http://www.pbismaryland.org/

Michigan Positive Behavior Support Network
http://www.bridges4kids.org/PBS/index.htm

Missouri Center on Schoolwide Positive Behavior Support
http://meta.missouri.edu/MUPBIS/index.html

New Hampshire Center for Effective Behavioral Interventions and Supports
http://www.nhcebis.seresc.net

New Jersey's PBSIS Project
http://www.njpbs.org/

Tennessee Schoolwide Positive Behavior Support
http://web.utk.edu/~swpbs/

References

Aburime, F. E. (2007). How manipulatives alter the mathematics achievement of students in Nigerian schools. *Educational Research Quarterly, 31*(1), 3–16.

Ardoin, S. P., Witt, J. C., Connel, J. E., & Koenig, J. L. (2005). Application of a three-tiered response to intervention model for instructional planning, decision making, and the identification of children in need of services. *Journal of Psychoeducational Assessment, 23,* 362–380.

Appelbaum, M. (2002). *How to talk to kids so they will listen.* Houston, TX: Appelbaum Training Institute.

Appelbaum, M. (2008). *How to handle the hard-to-handle student.* Thousand Oaks, CA: Corwin Press.

Aviles, C. B. (2001). Grading with norm-referenced or criterion-referenced measurements: To curve or not to curve, that is the question. *Social Work Education, 20*(5), 603–608.

Bambara, L. M., & Kern, L. (2005). *Individualized supports for students with problem behaviors: Designing positive behavior plans.* New York, NY: The Guilford Press.

Batsche, G. M. (2005, October). *Implementing the problem-solving/response to intervention protocols: Implications for school social workers.* Paper presented at the FASSW annual conference, Jacksonville, FL.

Bodie, G. D., Powers, W. G., & Fitch-Hauser, M. (2006). Chunking, priming, and active learning: Toward an innovative and blended approach to teaching communication-related skills. *Interactive Learning Environments, 14*(2), 119–135.

Bradley, R., Danielson, L., & Doolittle, J. (2007). Responsiveness to Intervention, 1997 to 2007. *Teaching Exceptional Children, 39*(5), 8–12.

Brophy, J. E. (1996). *Teaching problem students.* New York: Guilford Publishing.

Burns, M. K. (2005). Using incremental rehearsal to increase fluency of single-digit multiplication facts with children identified as learning disabled in mathematics computation. *Education and Treatment of Children, 28*(3), 237–249.

Cai, S. (2000). A content integrated approach in coping with college students' anxiety and depression. *Physical Educator, 57*(2), 69–77.

Chapman, M. (1995). Designing literacy learning experiences in a multiage classroom. *Language Arts, 72,* 416–428.

Chard, S. C. (1998). *The project approach: Making curriculum come alive.* New York: Scholastic.

Cheek, J. R., Bradley, L. J., Reynolds, J., & Coy, D. (2002). An intervention for helping elementary students reduce test anxiety. *Professional School Counseling, 6*(2), 162–165.

Christensen, L., Young, K. R., & Marchant, M. (2004). The effects of a peer-mediated positive behavior support program on socially appropriate classroom behavior. *Education and Treatment of Children, 27,* 199–234.

Christensen, L., Young, K. R., & Marchant, M. (2007). Behavioral intervention planning: Increasing appropriate behavior of a socially withdrawn student. *Education & Treatment of Children, 30*(4), 81–103.

Cipani, E. (1993). Non-compliance: Four strategies that work. CEC Mini Library: Classroom Management; *ERIC ED361973.*

Clark, S., Worcester, W., Dunlap, G., Murray, M., & Bradley-Klug, K. (2002). Using multiple measures to evaluate positive behavior support: A case example. *Journal of Positive Behavior Interventions, 3,* 131–145.

Connell, J. P., & Wellborn, J. G. (1991). Competence, autonomy, and relatedness: A motivational analysis of self-system processes. In M. Gunnar & L. A. Sroufe (Eds.) *Minnesota symposium on child psychology (22),* 43–77. Hillsdale, NJ: Erlbaum.

Cruey, G. (2006). *Response to intervention.* Retrieved September 27, 2007, from http://specialneedseducation.suite101.com/article.cfm/response_to_intervention

Csikszentmihalyi, M, Rathunde, K., & Whalen, S. (1993). *Talented teenagers: The roots of success and failure.* New York: Cambridge University Press.

Curtis, D. (2002). The power of projects. *Educational Leadership, 60,* 50–52.

Daly III, E. J., Martens, B. K., Barnet, D., Witt, J. C., & Olson, S. C. (2007). Varying intervention delivery in response to intervention: Confronting and resolving challenges with measurement, instruction, and intensity. *School Psychology Review, 36*(4), 562–581.

Daqi, L. (2007). Story mapping and its effects on the writing fluency and word diversity of students with learning disabilities. *Learning Disabilities: A Contemporary Journal, 5*(1), 77–93.

Davis, G. N., Lindo, E. J., & Compton, D. L. (2007). Children at risk for reading failure: Constructing an early screening measure. *Teaching Exceptional Children, 39*(5), 32–37.

DeJesus, H. P., Almeida, P., Teixeira-Dias, J. J., & Watts, M. (2007). Where learners' questions meet modes of teaching: A study of cases. *Research in Education, 78,* 1–20.

Denton, C., Vaughn, S., & Fletcher, J. M. (2003). Bringing research-based practice in reading intervention to scale. *Learning Disabilities: Research & Practice, 18*(3), 201–211.

Donabella, M. A., & Rule, A. C. (2008). Four seventh grade students who qualify for academic intervention services in mathematics learning multi-digit multiplication with the Montessori Checkerboard. *Teaching Exceptional Children, 4*(3), 1–28.

Dunlap, G., Kern, L., & Worchester, J. (2001). Applied behavior analysis and academic instruction. *Focus on Autism and Other Developmental Disabilities, 16,* 129–136.

Dunlap, G., Kern-Dunlap, L., Clark, S., & Robbins, F. R. (1991). Functional assessment, curricular revision, and severe behavior problems. *Journal of Applied Behavior Analysis, 24,* 387–397.

Eylon, B., & Linn, M. (1988). Learning and instruction: An examination of four research perspectives in science education. *Review of Educational Research, 58,* 251–301.

Fairbanks, S., Sugai, G., & Guardino, D. (2007). Response to intervention: Classroom behavior support in second grade. *Exceptional Children, 73*(3), 288–G.

Ferrari, J. R. (1994). Dysfunctional procrastination and its relationship with self-esteem, interpersonal dependency, and self-defeating behaviors. *Personality and Individual Differences, 11,* 673–679.

Firmin, M., Hwang, C., & Copella, M. (2004). Learned helplessness: The effect of failure on test-taking. *Education, 124*(4), 688–693.

Fisher, C., Berliner, D., Filby, N., Marliave, R., Cahen, L., & Dishaw, M. (1980). Teaching behaviors, academic learning time, and student achievement: An overview. In C. Denham & A. Lieberman (Eds.), *Time to Learn.* Washington, DC: National Institutes of Education.

Fisher, M. A. (2008). Protecting confidentiality rights: The need for an ethical practical model. *American Psychologist, 63*(1), 1–13.

Fletcher, J. M., Coulter, W. A., Reschly, D. J., & Vaughn, S. (2004). Alternative approaches to the definition and identification of learning disabilities: Some questions and answers. *Annals of Dyslexia, 54*(2), 304–331.

Fore III, C., Boon, R., Laweson, Sr., C., & Martin, C. (2007). Using curriculum-based measurement for formative instructional decision-making in basic mathematics skills. *Education, 128*(2), 324–332.

Foorman, B. R., Francis, D. J., Fletcher, J. M., Schatschneider, C., & Mehta, P. (1998). The role of instruction in learning to read: Preventing reading disabilities in at-risk children. *Journal of Educational Psychology, 90,* 37–55.

Foorman, B. R., & Torgesen, J. K. (2001). Critical elements of classroom and small-group instruction promote reading success in all children. *Learning Disabilities Research & Practice, 16,* 202–211.

Foos, P. W., & Fisher, R. P. (1998). Using tests as learning opportunities. *Journal of Educational Psychology, 80*(2), 179–183.

Francis, D. J., Shaywitz, S. E., Stuebing, K. K., Shaywitz, B. A., & Fletcher, J. M. (1996). Developmental lag versus deficit models of reading disability: A longitudinal, individual growth curves analysis. *Journal of Educational Psychology, 88,* 3–17.

Fuchs, D., & Fuchs, L. S. (2007). Introduction to response to intervention: What, why, and how valid is it? *Reading Research Quarterly, 41*(1), 93–99.

Fuchs, D., Fuchs, L. S., Mathes, P. G., & Simmons, D. C. (1997). Peer-assisted learning strategies: Making classrooms more responsive to diversity. *American Educational Research Journal, 34*(1), 174–206. Retrieved April 18, 2008, from http://www.promisingpractices.net/

Glasgow, N. A., & Hicks, C. D. (2003). *What successful teachers do: 91 research-based strategies for new and veteran teachers.* Thousand Oaks, CA: Corwin Press.

Gregory, G. H., & Chapman, C. (2002). *Differentiated instructional strategies: One size doesn't fit all.* Thousand Oaks, CA: Corwin Press.

Gunter, P. L., & Denny, R. K. (1996). Research issues and needs regarding teacher use of classroom management strategies. *Behavioral Disorders, 22,* 15–20.

Gunter, P. L., & Shores, R. E. (1995). On the move: Using teacher/student proximity to improve students' behavior. *Teaching Exceptional Children, 28*(1), 12–15.

Hallam, S., & Price, J. (1998). Can the use of background music improve the behaviour and academic performance of children with emotional and behavioural difficulties? *British Journal of Special Education, 25*(2), 88–92.

Hargreaves, A. (2000). Mixed emotions: Teachers' perceptions of their interactions with students. *Teaching and Education, 16,* 811–826.

Harry, B., & Klingner, J. (2007). Discarding the deficit model. *Educational Leadership, 64*(5), 16–21.

Harwell, J. M. (2001). *Complete learning disabilities handbook: Ready-to-use strategies and activities for teaching students with learning disabilities* (2nd ed.). San Francisco: Jossey-Bass.

Hawken, L. H., & Horner, R. H. (2003). Evaluation of a targeted intervention within a schoolwide system of behavior support. *Journal of Behavioral Education, 12*(3), 225–240.

Hock, M., & Mellard, D. (2005). Reading comprehension strategies for adult literacy outcomes. *Journal of Adolescent & Adult Literacy, 49*(3), 192–200.

Hoffman, J. (2002). Flexible grouping strategies in the multiage classroom. *Theory into Practice, 41,* 47–63.

Holloway, J. H. (2003). Sustaining experienced teachers. *Educational Leadership, 60*(8), 87–89.

Horner, R. H., & Day, H. M. (1991). The effects of response efficiency on functionally equivalent competing behaviors. *Journal of Applied Behavior Analysis, 24,* 719–732.

Horner, R. H., Day, H. M., Sprague, J. R., O'Brien, M., & Heathfield, L. T. (1991). Interspersed requests: A nonaversive procedure for reducing aggression and self-injury during instruction. *Journal of Applied Behavior Analysis, 24,* 265–278.

Hughes, J.N., Wen, L., Oi-Man, K., & Loyd, L.K. (2008). Teacher-student support, effortful engagement, and achievement: A 3-year longitudinal study. *Journal of Educational Psychology, 100*(1), 1–14.

Individuals With Disabilities Education Act (IDEA). (2004). Public Law 108-446.

Jenkins, J. R., & O'Connor, R. E. (2002). Early identification and intervention for young children with reading/learning disabilities. In R. Bradley, L. Danielson, & D. P. Hallahan (Eds.), *Identification of learning disabilities: Research to practice* (pp. 99–150). Mawah, NJ: Lawrence Erlbaum Associates.

Jenkins, J. R., Zumeta, R., Dupree, O., & Johnson, K. (2005). Measuring gains in reading ability with passage reading fluency. *Learning Disabilities Research & Practice, 20*(4), 245–253.

Jensen, E. (1998). *Teaching with the brain in mind.* Alexandria, VA: Association for Supervision and Curriculum Development.

Johnson, E., Mellard, D. F., Fuchs, D., & McKnight, M. A. (2006). *Responsiveness to intervention (RTI): How to do it.* Lawrence, KS: National Research Center on Learning Disabilities.

Kemp, K. A., & Eaton, M. A. (2008). *RTI: The classroom connection for literacy: Reading intervention and measurement.* Port Chester, NY: Dude Publishing.

Kendall, P. C., & Treadwell, K. R. H. (2007). The role of self-statements as a mediator in treatment for youth with anxiety disorders. *Journal of Consulting & Clinical Psychology, 75*(3), 380–389.

Kern, L. (1995). Functional analysis and intervention for breath holding. *Applied Behavior Analysis, 28*(3), 339–40.

Kern, L., Childs, K. E., Dunlap, G., Clarke, S., & Falk, G. D. (1994). Using an assessment-based curricular intervention to improve the classroom behavior of a student with emotional and behavioral challenges. *Journal of Applied Behavior Analysis, 27*, 7–19.

Kern, L., Choutka, C. M., & Sokol, N. G. (2002). Assessment-based antecedent interventions used in natural settings to reduce challenging behavior: An analysis of the literature. *Education and Treatment of Children, 25*(1), 113–130.

Kern, L., Koegel, R. L., Dyer, K., Blew, P. A., & Fenton, L. R. (1982). The effects of physical exercise on self-stimulation and appropriate responding in autistic children. *Journal of Autism and Developmental Disorders, 12*, 399–419.

Kern, L., Vorndran, C., Hilt, A., Ringdahl, J., Adelman, B., & Dunlap, G. (1998). Choice as an intervention to improve behavior: A review of the literature. *Journal of Behavioral Education, 8*, 151–169.

King-Sears, M. D., & Carpenter, S. L. (1997). *Teaching self-management to elementary students with developmental disabilities.* Washington, DC: American Association on Mental Retardation.

Knowles, M. S. (1986). *Using learning contracts.* San Francisco: Jossey-Bass.

Konrad, M., Fowler, C. H., Walker, A. R., Test, D. W., & Wood, W. M. (2007). Effects of self-determination interventions on the academic skills of students with learning disabilities. *Learning Disability Quarterly, 30*(2), 89–113.

Logan, P., & Skinner, C. (1998). Improving students' perceptions of a mathematics assignment by increasing problem completion rates: Is problem completion a reinforcing agent? *School Psychology Quarterly, 13*, 322–331.

Mace, A. B., Shapiro, E. S., & Mace, F. C. (1998). Effects of warning stimuli for reinforcer withdrawal and task onset on self-injury. *Journal of Applied Behavior Analysis, 31*, 679–682.

Mankins, M. C. (2004). Stop wasting valuable time. *Harvard Business Review, 82*(9), 58–65.

Marzano, R. J. (2003). *What works in schools: Translating research into action.* Alexandria, VA: Association for Supervision and Curriculum Development.

Marzano, R. J., Marzano, J., & Pickering, D. J. (2003). *Classroom management that works: Research-based strategies for every teacher.* Alexandria, VA: Association for Supervision and Curriculum Development.

Mason, D. A., Schroeter, D. D., Combs, R. K., & Washington, K. (1992). Assigning average-achieving eighth graders to advanced mathematics classes in urban junior high. *Elementary School Journal, 92*, 587–599.

Mathes, P. G., & Fuchs, D. (1997). Cooperative story mapping. *Remedial & Special Education, 18*(1), 20–28.

McCook, J. D. (2006). *The RTI guide: Developing and implementing a model in your schools.* Horsham, PA: LRP Publications.

McIntosh, K., Herman, K., Sanford, A., McGraw, K., & Florence, K. (2004). Teaching transitions. *Teaching Exceptional Children, 37*(1), 32–38.

McLaughlin, T. F., & Malaby, J. E. (1975). The effects of various token reinforcement contingencies on assignment completion and accuracy during variable and fixed token exchange schedules. *Canadian Journal of Behavioural Science, 7*(4), 411–419.

McMaster, K. L., Shu-Hsuan Kung, I., Insoon, H., & Cao, M. (2008). Peer-assisted learning strategies: A "Tier 1" approach to promoting English learners' response to intervention. *Exceptional Children, 74*(2), 194–214.

Mellard, D. F., & Johnson, E. (2008*). RTI: A practioner's guide to implementing response to intervention.* Thousand Oaks, CA: Corwin Press & NAESP.

Mills, R. (1998). Grouping students for instruction in middle schools. *ERIC Digest,* 19980601. (ERIC Document Reproduction Service No. ED4195631)

Montana Office of Public Instruction. (2008). RTI: Team problem solving. Retrieved February 28, 2008, from http://opi.mt.gov/PDF/SpecED/training/RTl/TeamProbSolve.pdf

Moore, B. M. (1988). Achievement in basic math skills for low-performing students: A study of teachers' affect and CAI. *Journal of Experimental Education, 57*(1), 38–44.

Morgan, R. L., Whorton, J. E., & Willets, J. (2000). Use of peer-mediation to develop instructional behavior in pre-service teachers. *College Student Journal, 34*(2), 146–155.

National Association of State Directors of Special Education, Inc. (2005). *Response to intervention: Policy considerations and implementation.* Alexandria, VA: Author.

National Reading Panel. (2000). *Report of the national reading panel: Teaching students to read: An evidence-based assessment of the scientific research literature on reading and its implications for reading instruction: Reports of the subgroups.* Bethesda, MD: National Institute of Child Health and Human Development, National Institutes of Health.

National Research Council on Learning Disabilities. (2008) *Professional development and collaboration within the RTI process.* Retrieved February 28, 2008, from http://www.nrcld.org/rti_practices/collaboration.html

Northey, S. S. (2005). *Handbook on differentiated instruction for middle and high schools.* Larchmont, NY: Eye on Education.

Paden, N., & Stell, R. (1997). Reducing procrastination through assignment and course design. *Marketing Education Review, 7*(2), 17–25.

Pemberton, J. B. (2003). Communicating academic progress as an integral part ofAssessment. *Teaching Exceptional Children, 35*(4), 16–20.

Pullen, P. C., Lane, H. B., Lloyd, J. W., Nowak, R., & Ryals, J. (2005). Effects of explicit instruction on decoding of struggling first grade students: A data-based case study. *Education and Treatment of Children,* 28, 63–76.

Rasinski, T., & Lenhart, L. (2008). Explorations of fluent readers. *Reading Today,* 25(3), 18.

Reichle, J., Drager, K., & Davis, C. (2002). Using request for assistance to obtain desired items and to gain release from nonpreferred activities: Implications for assessment and intervention. *Education and Treatment of Children,* 25, 47–66.

Reid, R., & Lienemann, T. O. (2006). *Strategy instructions for students with learning disabilities.* New York: The Guilford Press.

Reynolds, D., & Nicolson, R. I. (2007). Follow-up of an exercise-based treatment for children with reading difficulties. *Dyslexia, 13*(2), 78–96.

Roberts, M. S., & Semb, G. B. (1989). Student selection of deadline conditions in a personalized psychology course. *Teaching of Psychology, 16*(3), 128–130.

Riley-Tillman, T. C., Kalberer, S. M., & Chafouleas, S. M. (2005). Selecting the right tool for the job: A review of behavior monitoring tools used to assess student response to intervention. *California School Psychologist, 10*, 81–91.

Sargent, J. (2001). *Data Retreat Facilitator's Guide*. Naperville, IL: NCREL.

Serok, S. (1991). The application of Gestalt methods for the reduction of test anxiety in students. *Assessment & Evaluation in Higher Education, 16*(2), 157–165.

Sheets, R. H., & Gay, G. (1996). Student perceptions of disciplinary conflict in ethnically diverse classrooms. *NASSP Bulletin, 80*, 84–93.

Shinn, M. R. (2007). Identifying students at risk: Monitoring performance, and determining eligibility within response to Intervention: Research on educational need and benefit from academic intervention. *School Psychology Review, 36*(4), 5.

Shulman, R. (1993). Developing thinking skills with task cards. *Teaching PreK–8, 23*(5), 56–59.

Siegel Robertson, J. (2000). Is attribution training a worthwhile classroom intervention for K–12 students with learning difficulties? *Educational Psychology Review, 12*(1), 111–134.

Snow, C. E., Burns, M. S., & Griffin, P. (1998). *Preventing reading difficulties in young children*. Washington, DC: National Acadamies Press.

Snow, D. R. (2005). *Classroom strategies for helping at-risk students*. Alexandria, VA: Association for Supervision and Curriculum Development.

Stecker, P. M. (2007). Tertiary intervention. *Teaching Exceptional Children, 39*(5), 50–57.

Stahl, S. A., & Fairbanks, M. M. (1986). The effects of vocabulary instruction: A model-based meta-analysis. *Review of Educational Research, 56*(1), 72–110.

Sullivan, M. (1993). A meta-analysis of experimental research studies based on the Dunn & Dunn learning styles model and its relationship to academic achievement and performance. Doctoral dissertation, St. John's University, Jamaica, NY.

Tanner, J. F., & Roberts, J. A. (1996). Active learning: Students as teachers. *Marketing Education Review, 6*, 41–46.

Thompson, R. A., & Wyatt, J. M. (1999). Current research on child maltreatment: Implications for educators. *Educational Psychology Review, 11*(3), 173–201.

Tomlinson, C. A. (2001*). How to differentiate instruction in mixed-ability classrooms* (2nd ed.). Alexandria, VA: Association for Supervision and Curriculum Development.

Torgesen, J. K. (2001). Intensive remedial instruction for children with severe reading disabilities: Immediate and long-term outcomes from two instructional approaches. *Journal of Learning Disabilities, 34*, 33–58.

Umbreit, J., Ferro, J., Liaupsin, C. J., & Lane, K. L. (2007). *Functional behavioral assessment and function-based intervention: An effective, practical approach*. Upper Saddle River, NJ: Pearson Education.

Van Overwalle, F., & De Metsenaere, M. (1990). The effects of attribution-based intervention and study strategy training on academic achievement in college freshmen. *British Journal of Educational Psychology, 60*, 299–311.

Vaughn, S., & Klingner, J. K. (1999). Teaching reading comprehension through collaborative strategic reading. *Intervention in School & Clinic, 34*(5), 284–293.

Vaughn, S., & Roberts, G. (2007). Secondary interventions in reading. *Teaching Exceptional Children, 39*(5), 40–46.

Wasley, P., Hampel, R., & Clark, R. (1997). *Kids and school reform.* San Francisco: Jossey-Bass.

Wedl, R. J. (2005). *Response to intervention: An alternative to traditional eligibility criteria for students with disabilities.* Minneapolis, MN: Center for Policy Studies and Hamline University.

Wilkins, A. (2002). Colored overlays and their effects on reading speed: A review. *Opthalmic and Physiological Optics, 22*(5), 448–454.

William, D., Lee, C., Harrison, C., & Black, P. (2004). Teachers developing assessment for learning: Impact on student achievement. *Assessment in Education: Principles, Policy & Practice, 11*(1), 49–65.

Woodward, J. (2006). Developing automaticity in multiplication facts: Integrating strategy instruction with timed practice drills. *Learning Disability Quarterly, 29*(4), 269–289.

Wright, J. (2007). *RTI toolkit: A practical guide for schools.* Port Chester, NY: Dude Publishing.

Wubbles, T., Brekelmans, M., Van Tartwijk, J., & Admiral, W. (1999). Interpersonal relationships between teachers and students in the classroom. In H. C. Waxman & H. J. Walberg (Eds.), *New directions for teaching practice and research* (pp. 151–170). Berkeley, CA: McCutchan Publishing.

Zimmerman, B. J., & Ringle, J. (1981). Effects of model persistence and statements of confidence on children's self-efficacy and problem solving. *Educational Psychology, 73*(4), 485–493.

Index

The letter f refers to a figure.

CORWIN PRESS

The Corwin Press logo—a raven striding across an open book—represents the union of courage and learning. Corwin Press is committed to improving education for all learners by publishing books and other professional development resources for those serving the field of PreK–12 education. By providing practical, hands-on materials, Corwin Press continues to carry out the promise of its motto: **"Helping Educators Do Their Work Better."**

Appelbaum
Training Institute

Appelbaum Training Institute (ATI) provides the latest, the best, and the most research-based information on the most current subjects in a fun and enjoyable manner through professional development, training, and resources to educators and parents of children of all ages and diverse backgrounds. The ATI motto is **"Building Bridges to the Future,"** and that is exactly what the Appelbaum Training Institute does every day in every way for educators across the world.